Work Better. Save The Planet

The Earth-First Workplace Is Good For People, Great For Business.

LISA WHITED

In memory of Fritz Steele, PhD

TABLE OF CONTENTS

INTRODUCTION

In the 21st century world, post-pandemic and staring down the barrel of catastrophic climate change, your father's office is no longer fit for purpose. The obsolete workplace is bad for business, problematic for people, and harmful to the environment. Your employees and our planet demand better. If you begin the process, now, of bringing your workspace into the future while engaging your employees so they own the change, you'll build a stronger, more engaged, and ultimately, more profitable business. There is no time to lose.

This book contains a process to use when considering the purpose of your office after the worldwide pandemic of 2020. The PLLANET model includes 7 tenets that, when used together, are proven to result in higher employee engagement, more efficient use of space, and a more inclusive workplace. The 7 tenets work in concert so that your stakeholders (employees, managers, and leaders) have greater buy-in of the resulting change. This book is written for the world we are in now. A world with:

- catastrophic climate change
- a renewed focus on diversity, belonging and inclusion
- a higher likelihood of remote and hybrid working

This book is primarily intended for knowledge workers – also known as white collar workers – although there are aspects that apply to other types of workers. The audience for this book is C-suite executives, HR professionals, facility and real estate professionals, managers, employees, and anyone interested in making a positive difference for their people, their organization, and the planet.

Disengaged and stressed employees

The Gallup Poll, which measures people's engagement with work, has regularly shown that people are not happy at work. As of 2021, 80% worldwide and 66% of office workers in the U.S. were either highly disengaged or disengaged with their work.[1] "Highly disengaged" are the people who are going to work every day but are on Monster.com looking for a new job. You are paying them to do work for you while they search for work elsewhere. People are also suffering stress, mental crisis, higher rates of addiction and depression – much of which can be tied to their disengagement at work and to concern about climate change.[2]

Frustrations with the office

Prior to 2020, every day of the week, a large percentage of white-collar workers arrived at the office and were annoyed. They were frequently distracted by noise and interruptions. They struggled to find quiet places to focus or appropriate spaces in which to have meetings and conduct collaborative work with colleagues, as shown in *figure #1*. I know, because in 2019 I surveyed 5,500 employees who overwhelmingly cited these factors as the greatest barriers to their productivity.[3]

Prior to my survey, I read through two decades of data from organizations that indicated the same complaints—noise, distractions, interruptions, and a lack of quiet places to work, coupled with being too hot or too cold, were consistently at the top of the complaint list.

And then in 2020 the pandemic hit, and everyone went home. Now we sit poised before a great opportunity. It is time to change the way, and the places, in which we work.

53%

Distractions From
People Interrupting

45%

Lack of Quiet Areas
Away from Distraction

48%

Distraction
from Noise

Figure #1: Employees primary complaints about the office based upon 5,500 respondents

Impact on the climate

Air travel, commuting, building operations and construction impose a significant negative impact on the climate; commercial buildings contribute 39% of global carbon emissions.[4] The United Nation's Sixth Assessment Report of the Intergovernmental Panel on Climate Change (IPCC) [5] opens with, "It is unequivocal that human influence has warmed the atmosphere, ocean and land. Widespread and rapid changes in the atmosphere, ocean, cryosphere and biosphere have occurred."[6] The IPCC Report makes it clear that we have a choice: we can be resigned to a doomsday scenario of a hot planet, or we can do everything in our power to keep the warming at or below 1.5 degrees Celsius.[7]

Working from home experiment

When COVID-19 and the lockdown hit, people abruptly scattered to their houses for a great and unplanned home-working experiment. Zoom fatigue soon followed, with employees complaining of back-to-back online video meetings and an inability to separate their personal lives from their work lives. Work invaded their living rooms, dining rooms and bedrooms. Their family and personal time spilled over into their meetings and work activities. The boundaries that used to exist – separated by a commute or a physical change of location – evaporated. Those that had young children to home school or older relatives to care for were stretched beyond reasonable expectations. Most people felt overwhelmed, frustrated, and stressed.

Several months in, some employees pined for a return to how things used to be in the office. That loud, disruptive workplace now seemed like a heavenly sanctuary after being confined in small abodes with flat mates and family week after week. Did people forget how the office negatively impacted their productivity and their engagement? Memories of meeting room scarcity and spotty Wi-Fi seemed like faded color photographs from a long-ago family vacation.

Empty offices

An aspect of work that is not as well known by the average worker but is recognized by facility management and real estate professionals, is that well before COVID-19, offices were empty 40% to 60% of the time.[8] Utilization studies measure how often a space is occupied either through the use of sensors or measured manually by counting how many people are at desks 5 to 6 times a day over a two-week period.

Across varied industries and geographies, we know that many people were not sitting at their desks 8 hours a day. They did not need to sit in one place because today's technology permits mobility and flexibility that was not available before the 1990s and 2000s. For the past 15 years, employees have readily moved from meeting rooms to cafés to clients' offices to coffee shops, while their assigned desk sits empty for hours at a time. What this means is that large office buildings have pockets of empty space for thousands of hours a year. As the chart in *figure 2* shows, many office spaces were utilized only 63% of the time. Again, all this was happening well before the pandemic. This empty space is wasteful and cost ineffective for business. A further consideration, tied to global warming, is the contribution that commercial buildings make to global carbon emissions because of the construction process and due to daily facility operations like lights, heating, and air conditioning.[9]

Our offices were created based upon an Industrial Revolution model when people had to leave their homes to travel to the factory to stand hunched over a machine all day long. We have not needed to work this way for decades, but we have acted as if being tethered to a singular desk is a requirement to doing one's work.

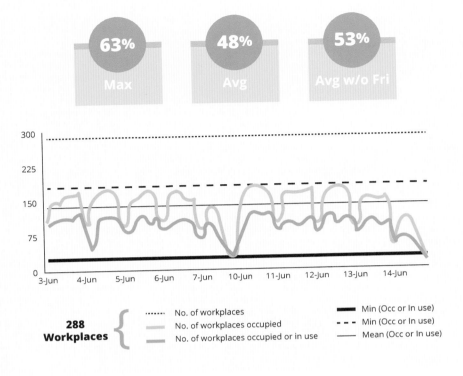

Figure #2: Typical utilization results; a chart showing occupancy rates at 288 desks across a 2-week period

To summarize, there are three important takeaways from this review of current workplace practices:

1. A great majority of people have been disengaged with work for twenty years, which has a detrimental impact on performance and productivity.

2. Employees have complained about aspects of the office for a long time.

3. Office desks have been empty 40% to 60% of the time, leading to a massive waste of money in both real estate and operating costs.

Given these issues, why would we want to return to 'normal'? This is an opportune time to make improvements that are better for people, better for business, and better for the planet.

Workplace transformation

A reimagined way of working can unite people, inspire innovation, energize employees and be less harmful to the planet. We can build community and save the planet if we are courageous enough to not go back to 'the old normal'.

For more than 20 years I have worked with organizations to create workplaces where people cannot wait to get to work every day. My approach to this work has evolved as my professional career and education has evolved, and in that time, I've perfected my own Venn diagram of success: HR (people), facilities (space) and organizational leadership (vision) *(figure #3)*. The overlap of these three is what I call the sweet spot of workplace transformation: it takes conversations between, and with, the three realms (HR, facilities management/real estate, and the C-suite) to bring about truly successful workplace transformation.

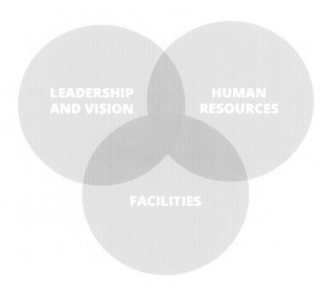

Figure #3: Venn diagram showing the sweet spot of workplace transformation – when leadership/vision, HR and Real Estate/Facilities collaborate

I have used the PLLANET process shared in this book successfully with numerous organizations and thousands of their employees. You can create a workplace that inspires innovation, engages employees, creates authentic connections, and builds community at work. There is a way to use office space more wisely, to save a lot of money on overhead costs and to make choices that can help slow climate change and positively impact people's wellbeing. I'm going to show you how.

A Note About Case Studies

Proven, successful methods are outlined in the following chapters. Each chapter closes with a case study that you can share with your colleagues as you work to build community and engagement through the change process. The case studies have had identifying features changed and have been expanded to demonstrate how the 7 tenets can be applied in a situation. Throughout the book you will find pragmatic exercises with step-by-step detail, allowing you or anyone on your team to be successful with the different tenets.

THE 7 PLLANET TENETS

The 7 PLLANET Tenets bring about positive workplace change. These tenets can inspire innovation, engage employees, create authentic connections, and build community at work – all while using less space, which not only saves money, but gives us a fighting chance to make a dent in neutralizing climate change.

Many organizations say they want to put their people first. It could be surmised that putting people first – considering our own individual needs over the needs of the environment – has led to the abysmal state of our climate. The 7 PLLANET tenets address the needs of people but puts the Earth at the center of the process.

It requires courage to reconsider the notion of work and the workplace. Are you willing to challenge the status quo? Brave enough to speak up and question embedded assumptions? Do you have the desire to imagine new ways of working? Now you have a guide to support you in charting a future into brave, innovative ways of working.

COVID-19 has been a terrible, disruptive event that has negatively impacted most of the world and killed millions of people. The impact on our economy will be long-lasting. Understandably, people want to return to a sense of normalcy. For many people, normalcy means heading back to the office.

Purpose
Clarify purpose before embarking on a transformation to create a touchstone for successful decision-making and communication.

Language
Use consistent, agreed upon and clear terminology as an essential part of initiating effective change.

Less
Commit to less space than you've been used to, to support effective working.

Ask
Invite people to a conversation about change in an intentional and inclusive manner so that community and connection are built into the process.

Net Zero
Create carbon neutral ways of working by first understanding how offices have typically been designed and built, which lets you respectfully challenge embedded assumptions to create a different experience for employees, and ultimately, impact climate change.

Equity
Include the voices of the marginalized and underrepresented in your process. Intentionally build equity through architecture and design.

Time
Act now and take the positive lessons learned through the working-from-home experience to reimagine work and the workplace to benefit our planet.

Why wouldn't we welcome going back to the status quo after the worldwide pandemic everyone has been through? Why not simply return to our "normal" way of working and interacting with colleagues, settling into the way things always were? Because this moment is your opportunity to change your workplace. The time is now to reconsider the purpose of the office and correct many of the inefficiencies and problems that existed in your work world before the pandemic. Seize upon this moment to hit pause and change your office trajectory. People's wellbeing and that of the Earth depends upon acting now.

We spend so much of our lives working. By using the process in this book, you can impact Gallup's statistic of 80% of people being disengaged. Let's reimagine work, reignite employees, and recalibrate your workplace so our collective future is brighter and our planet cleaner.

EMPLOYEES dislike change and emotionally connect with their workplaces as strongly as they do their homes and families. However, they need workplaces to change because they are bored, over-commuting and uninspired, all of which means unhappy and less productive employees.

THE PLANET needs workplaces to change because workplaces play a crucial role in climate change.

Because of the pandemic, now is the time for that change.

How the 7 PLLANET Tenets were created

It was 2009 and I had been collaborating with a technology firm for eight months to design and plan a renovation for 60 of their employees, a software engineering team. Previously, the engineers had been working in a dark space with minimal natural light. The office was straight out of the comic strip "Dilbert": a maze of high, grey-walled cubicles. Not only did the company leaders want to bring the office interior into the 21st century, but they also wanted to connect employees more efficiently across functional areas.

During this project, I had worked closely with two managers as we determined the best configurations for their employees. The staff were often engrossed in deep-thinking work, yet needed to easily connect and brainstorm software solutions. The employees had just moved into the renovated office, and I was visiting to see how people were adapting.

Bright sunlight streamed through the large windows. White furniture cut crisp lines against the deep oranges and vibrant greens splashed on the walls. There was an atmosphere of humming productivity among the thirty or so people quietly working at their computers.

I ran into one of the managers, who was sitting with his team in the sunlit space. He greeted me with a grin – "Lisa, the team loves the space! They have embraced the open and connected layout and love the private rooms for quiet work."

I walked further down the hallway and saw the other manager sitting behind her desk in her office with a furrowed brow. "Hey, Amelia, how is your team finding the new office?" I asked.

She looked up, slowly shaking her head. Her face already told the story. "I'm sorry to say the guys are frustrated. They're not at all happy with their new space."

I walked away confused. I could hear the tension in her voice. How could one team be so happy, and the other so miserable, when the spaces and amenities were virtually identical? I walked further into the office and saw four people in one of the meeting rooms, gathered around a white board. My mind still puzzling over the dilemma of a happy team and a neighboring frustrated team, I considered what could have caused the uneven outcome. As I reached the end of the hallway, reflecting on the opposite reactions – and on where I saw the managers sitting (one among his people and the other squirreled away in her office), I realized what had gone wrong. And that realization changed everything about how I approached workplace design.

A Revamped Process

Within the year, I had not only figured out how to create more equitable and predictable experiences for my clients' employees, but I had built a framework that allowed employees to be successful with one of the greatest challenges in the office: workplace change. I continued to use the framework for several years and, in 2020, as I became more passionate about climate change, I reinvented the framework as 7 tenets called "PLLANET."

It is always best practice to conduct pre- and post-change surveys to see if goals are being met. Typically, a pre-change survey is issued to all employees very early in the planning process. A post-change survey is issued 2 or 3 months after the change has occurred.

When I started applying the revamped workplace change method the pre-and post-survey scores improved by significant margins. (*Figure 4*). The realization I came to during that project forms the basis of this book.

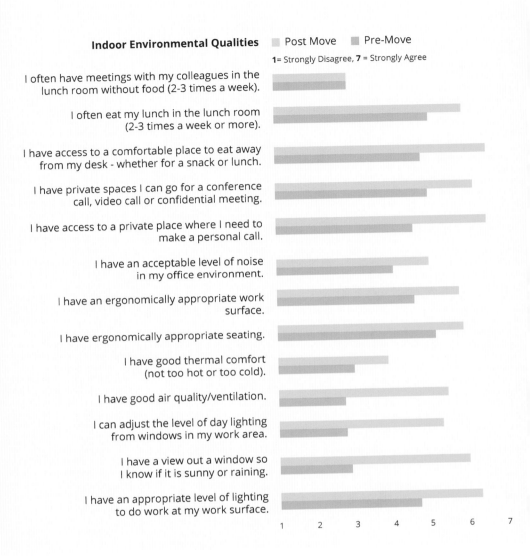

Indoor Environmental Qualities   ■ Post Move   ■ Pre-Move

1= Strongly Disagree, **7** = Strongly Agree

I often have meetings with my colleagues in the lunch room without food (2-3 times a week).

I often eat my lunch in the lunch room (2-3 times a week or more).

I have access to a comfortable place to eat away from my desk - whether for a snack or lunch.

I have private spaces I can go for a conference call, video call or confidential meeting.

I have access to a private place where I need to make a personal call.

I have an acceptable level of noise in my office environment.

I have an ergonomically appropriate work surface.

I have ergonomically appropriate seating.

I have good thermal comfort (not too hot or too cold).

I have good air quality/ventilation.

I can adjust the level of day lighting from windows in my work area.

I have a view out a window so I know if it is sunny or raining.

I have an appropriate level of lighting to do work at my work surface.

Figure #4: Survey results showing pre and post workplace change comparison

That visit to my technology client's office underscored the challenge of creating a positive outcome for people as they experience workplace change. Ironically, the reason that workplace change can be difficult is because the people most impacted by the change – frontline employees – are often left out of conversations because workplace leaders are literally concerned about "managing expectations." Talk about a paradox!

Stress

With so many people experiencing change at different levels and rates of acceptance, it can seem almost impossible to promise a successful and evenly distributed outcome. As a leader, you are concerned about disappointing your people when they can't have everything they put on their wish list – I get it. The last thing you want to do is let your people down, so it might seem easier to not ask and risk raising their expectations. Yet, people relish the opportunity to discuss what could be better for them – what might allow them to do their best work. When you are considering workplace change you have an opportunity that shouldn't be wasted. Your opportunity is to give your employees a safe space – in a well-facilitated manner – to share their thoughts and suggestions.

People experience high levels of stress at work and, according to the American Psychological Association, workplace stress is the third most common source of stress following money.[10] If people are already stressed at work, it seems to reason that asking them to undergo workplace change might cause greater anxiety.

The American Institute of Stress is a non-profit organization founded in 1978. Stress has become such an ingrained part of our vocabulary and daily existence, that it is difficult to believe that our current use of the term originated a little more than 60 years ago, when it was essentially "coined" by Hans Selye, who founded the Institute.[11]

The Institute claims workplace stress levels do not come from the job itself, but from the person-environment fit.[12] Some individuals thrive in the time urgent pressure cooker of life in the fast lane, having to perform several duties at the same time and a list of things to do that would overwhelm most of us — provided they perceive that they are in control. They would be severely stressed by dull, dead-end assembly line work enjoyed by others who shun responsibility and simply want to perform a task that is well within their capabilities. [13]

Stress is a highly personalized phenomenon and can vary widely to a person even in identical situations for different reasons. One survey showed that having to complete paperwork was more stressful for many police officers than the dangers associated with pursuing criminals. The severity of job stress depends on the magnitude of the demands that are being made and the individual's sense of control or decision-making latitude they have in dealing with those demands. Scientific studies based on this model confirm that workers who perceive they are subjected to high demands but have little control are at increased risk for cardiovascular disease.[14]

An individual's sense of control – what they feel they can control in their workplace or about their work – correlates to a higher or lesser level of stress.

We also know that our fear of losing motivates us more than the prospect of gaining something of equal value. [15] *(figure #5)* This is called loss aversion. If I lose $20, I will feel it more deeply than I will experience a $20 win. Therefore, even if you are creating the most spectacular office with all the bells and whistles you can imagine, employees will still feel anxious about the change. What they know (the old office) is comforting. The unknown (new office) is uncharted territory and therefore discomforting.

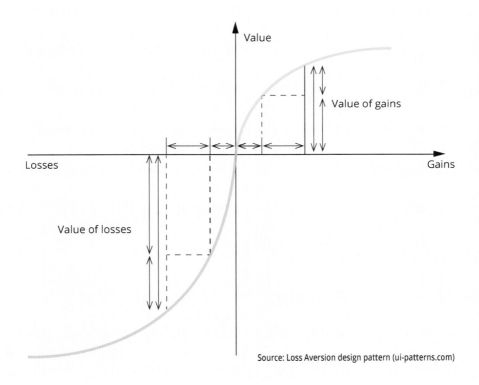

Source: Loss Aversion design pattern (ui-patterns.com)

Figure #5: People experience loss at a greater level than an equal gain

Thinking back to the software technology office discussed earlier, the goal had been met successfully: a light-filled modern office that gave software engineers a variety of places to work, including spaces for quiet, focused thinking. Yet some of the employees were still unhappy. My realization on the day of my visit was that you cannot simply successfully arrive at the project goals; you need to bring everyone on the trip.

Why Change At Work is Difficult

Most change theories include a step to involve people in conversations about the change, yet often that interaction happens too late in the workplace change process, and it is limited to a sub-group of "change champions" rather than the entire organization. What I mean by "too late", is that the physical design of a space cannot be completed in a bubble without input from those who will use the workspace. The workers most impacted by the change are the ones best suited to share what could work better for them.

Change management models typically include these five steps.[16]

1. Prepare the organization for change
2. Craft a vision and plan for change
3. Implement the change
4. Embed changes within company culture and practices
5. Review progress and analyze results

Despite decades of research and attention to change management, there is a perception that change is hard, and that most change efforts fail.[17, 18]

When it comes to the workplace, what most change theories are missing is the fact that people are emotionally attached to their workplace and gain their identity through the work they do. Work consumes a tremendous portion of their waking hours. How they feel about their work causes a ripple effect that impacts those around them – their partners, children, family, and friends – and even their neighbors.

Simply applying the best practices of change theory won't cut it in your workplace. If best practices worked, more than the current 20% of the population would be engaged in their work. What is needed is a workplace reformation – even better – a workplace revolution. I created the 7 PLLANET tenets because I want to launch a workplace revolution that will help people be more engaged with their work, which positively impacts productivity for the business, and would positively impact the planet.

We falsely think that people will go along with change at work. Regarding people and change, how often have you heard employer comments like these:

"If they don't like it, they can leave."

"They are lucky to have a job; they'll deal with it."

"Let's just get on with it."

"Build it and they will come."

But the simple truth is that the people most impacted by the proposed change are often the last to hear about it. And this simple truth has a direct impact on whether your workplace transformation is successful. Employees are rarely invited into a meaningful conversation that could positively impact the outcome and create ownership of the result. Instead of being engaged in the change, they are fearful, resistant, or downright combative. They are freaked out because they feel left out. It doesn't have to be this way.

Instead of cherry picking who is included in meetings about workplace change, invite all employees into the conversation from the beginning of the initiative – not after the idea has been fully (or even halfway) baked. You will create a motivated, engaged group who feel pride and ownership of the result. As company leadership, it is up to you – and it is your responsibility to see this happens.

Remember, people's identities are directly tied to their work and their workplace. Including only a few voices in conversations about change leaves out a huge segment of impacted people and negatively reflects on their workplace experience.

When I began to consistently use the 7 PLLANET tenets, the findings from before and after (pre and post change surveys) resulted in a dramatic increase in positive metrics related to happiness, productivity and ownership.

There are many theories about change, but the reality of applying real change at work requires a process that recognizes your employees' ego and identity with their work and the workplace, and engages them with the ultimate purpose of their work.

In a post-COVID-19 world, you have the added challenge of reimagining what the workplace is for. Why have an office when so much work can be done outside of the office, working at home, free from the distractions and noise that the office was known for before lockdown? That challenge is an opportunity, and one of the greatest reasons we have for adopting new ways of working that will make a positive impact on climate change.

As challenging as workplace change is, know that successful outcomes are possible. If you use the 7 PLLANET tenets to engage employees, improve productivity, and build community with your employees, the benefits will be substantial. And, when designed thoughtfully, your business will recognize significant cost savings while having a positive impact on the planet.

PURPOSE

The first step to implementing successful workplace change is to clarify and align the PURPOSE of the change to the whole group. Your purpose is a clearly articulated vision that is widely shared with all employees and becomes a touchstone for decision-making and communication. Just as strategic planning is an iterative process, so, too, may your vision and purpose evolve over time.

Vision, Mission and Purpose are often conflated. The terms, as used in this text, are defined as:

Purpose – the difference we want to make in the world; it is our "why"

Vision – how the world will look once our purpose is fulfilled

Mission – what we do every day to help us reach our vision; it is the "how" or "what" we do to achieve our vision

A financial services company was going to relocate its headquarters such that people's commutes would quadruple. One of the primary drivers for the change was recruitment. The CEO's vision was clear in his mind – to create a workplace that was a destination, where people couldn't wait to get to work, and where he would have an abundance of qualified candidates for open positions. He skillfully clarified his purpose for the move, brought the rest of his leadership team and all employees into the vision conversation early in the discussions, and used the change as an opportunity to galvanize his people toward the final goal.

The power of vision

There are hundreds of books and articles about why vision matters in organizations. Transitioning to a new way of working requires the same sort of attention: a widely shared, clearly articulated vision.

When participating in the "Headline Exercise" where people imagine they are reading the front page of a newspaper published 15 or 20 years into the future (a detailed explanation of the exercise is included in this chapter) invariably the conversation turns to sustainability and climate change. I have seen similar "front pages" created by employees involved in technology, insurance, banking, law, construction, NGOs, and environmental science.

When I have private meetings with CEOs and COOs and we talk about what they want their legacy to be, many times they mention their grandchildren and the world they hope they will inhabit in the future.

If the future of our planet is an issue people care deeply about, it is relatively easy to create a short, succinct vision that articulates their envisioned future. Whether it is a group of four people or 20, people often have far more in common with each other than not when they imagine how they want to make a difference.

Clarifying vision and articulating your purpose is the single most important tenet in PLLANET. If you skip this step at the beginning, you seriously jeopardize achieving your goals.

I've believed in the importance of visioning for decades, since I first experienced the power of writing down goals at the age of 18, forgot about the goals, and then discovered that list a few years later, amazed to find that all the items I'd listed had come true. In the 1981 entry, I had imagined my ideal day and focused on the type of work I would do, the car I would drive and the person I would marry. At age 26, I came across that journal page (titled, "My Ideal Day in 5 Years") and chuckled to myself that I had described my future so well – it had come about even though the actual journal had long been forgotten.

I was born with poor eyesight. When I was young my grandmother showed me how I could look through the hole in a cracker and the fuzziness would disappear. Many years later when I was reflecting on strategic planning and vision, I remembered my grandmother's advice. When you look through the hole in a Saltine cracker, extraneous things are blocked out, so you only see what you need to focus on. (*figure #6*) Vision clarification gets rid of the extras, so you focus on what is essential.

Figure #6: A grandmother's advice: Looking through the holes of a cracker can make things more clear

Vision and purpose are critical to pay attention to when attempting change and engaging people in transformation. Dan Pink's *Drive: The Surprising Truth About What Motivates Us* shares how purpose is an intrinsic human motivator.[19] Studies also show the importance to people in finding purpose-driven work – many are willing to forego higher salaries when they know their work is connected to a higher purpose. Employees want to know they are making a positive difference with their work.

Here are two specific exercises for clarifying vision that I love to use when working with individuals or groups to help them focus on what is important.

Headline Exercise

This exercise is a great small group endeavor for 2 or 3 people – but is equally rewarding for individuals. You imagine that it is 20 years into the future, 20XX. An article has just been published in an international newspaper about a change that has happened in the world. You know that this change came about because of your involvement with the organization/company 20 years prior.

What is the headline? What would be on the top half (above the fold) of the front page that would make you feel proud, that resonates with your own values? Create a cover image, headline, photos/drawings, charts/graphs with captions and a short story. Use a piece of flip chart paper, or use a Power Point slide as your "newspaper." *Figure #7* is an example for you to reference – but use your creativity – you do not need to follow the template.

Each group should have no more than 20 minutes to work on this exercise. The key is to focus on the conversations about the future more so than the visual merit of the final output. Each group shares their headline with the larger group, with an eye (or ear) towards finding common themes and threads. The commonalities of each headline will provide insight to the larger group's values and vision for the future, concluding with the creation of a memorable vision statement. A final distillation of the thoughts into one succinct statement is often best assigned to one person or a very small group. The vision statement should be brief – a sentence or phrase that anyone can recite without having to read off of a screen or paper. The simpler, the better.

Invite all employees to participate in the Headline Exercise – not just the leadership team. It is powerful to see a roomful of headline exercises and recognize the commonality from paper to paper. This is one way to create a purpose-driven vision where all voices are heard.

This exercise can easily be adapted to virtual groups as well – whether you use a Google Slide, a Power Point slide, or other online collaboration tool, a positive collaboration is (virtually) guaranteed.

CORPORATE REAL ESTATE NO LONGER ABOUT BRICK & MORTAR

Re-lease or repurpose real estate: Funneling savings into employees and other business needs & activities

Strategy is a blend of business technologies community and places.

Successfully engaged our employees in making those decisions

How one international corporation made different decisions about where/how work is done around the world based upon local culture and workplace preferences

Figure #7: Example output from Headline Exercise

Letter to Future Self

This exercise is inspired by *The Art of Possibility* by Rosamund Stone Zander and Benjamin Zander.

With as much detail as you can muster, describe a day in the future – from the moment you wake up in the morning until the minute you turn off the light at night. Describe your surroundings, what you are doing, reading, eating, who you are seeing, talking with, and connected to. Describe the type of work you are doing, what you are wearing, where you walk or drive or bicycle – no detail is too small for this exercise, in fact the more specific the details the better. Think about what is going well for you in this future view; you are writing from a place of possibility.

You are the only one who will read the letter – so be specific about what you hope for yourself in the next 6 months or 2 years – you define the time frame (and, as mentioned, in workplace change, I have participants use the expected completion date of the project). Then, tuck it away and make a note on your calendar to pull it out on a designated day.

When that day comes, as you read your letter back to yourself, make notes about what has happened or not happened. Consider if what you wrote is still important to you or if your goals or wishes have changed.

I have used this exercise with fifth graders, with recently retired folks, and with all ages in between. For the grade school kids, I have them place their letters in an envelope, address it to their home address and seal the envelope. I keep the letters in a safe place until they are seniors in high school and then mail the letters to their homes. Over the years, several have dropped me notes to let me know how their letters rang true to what they were now headed to study or to do after graduation.

With workplace change projects, I have people place the letters in self-addressed envelopes, collect them, and mail the letters upon project completion. This is a simple way to engage people in imagining how the proposed change may positively impact their future.

Connection to purpose is paramount

Now we have established that purpose and vision need to be a constant reminder and kept "front and center" in organizations and at the forefront of any workplace transformation. But how is that done well?

Once the vision or purpose is clear, it doesn't do much good if it is printed on a strategic plan document only seen by the executive team. Purpose must be shared widely and made visible to have a positive impact on people. And it is truly more successful if it is an inclusive, all-stakeholder-engaged exercise (as the Headline Exercise can be.)

Here are 6 ways to make purpose more visible.

1. Tie your organizational purpose to communications and messaging about workplace change. For example, if you are transitioning to shared, unassigned seating to support hybrid working, then when you tell people that they will be sharing a desk when they return to the office, use it as an opportunity to remind people of the organizational vision. For example, let's use a famous company's vision: "To make the best products on earth, and to leave the world better than we found it." An announcement about a transition to agile seating might begin, "We are making the best products on earth and want to leave the world better than we found it. To that end, we are introducing agile seating because this way of working will allow us to be nimbler and more responsive (quickly put together and dismantle product teams) and allows us to occupy less real estate. Commercial buildings contribute 39% of carbon emissions, and by reducing our physical footprint, we will be reducing our carbon footprint."

2. Identify a wall in your space to create a visible connection to purpose (we call them story walls.) These walls are not for "bragging" to clients about your great work. And it is not the mission statement printed in bold letters. Instead, story walls are specifically designed for your current (and prospective) employees. They highlight how you are making a difference in the world with your work and your values. A story wall is the result of a creative and inquisitive discovery process that gets to the heart of what the organization is trying to achieve. If you have done a thorough job clarifying your vision and purpose, then it is worth the time and investment to hire a talented graphic designer or visual storyteller to express that purpose in a creative and artful way as a physical manifestation of purpose. *Figure #8* shows images of story walls.

3. At the beginning of each gathering/meeting/town hall, keep the purpose front and center. Write it at the top of meeting agendas. Make it the first slide in your deck. Paste it in the chat. Say it aloud. Find relevant opportunities with your talking points to tie the topic to purpose.

4. State your organizational vision at the top of your Working Together Agreement (WTA). The WTA (explained in detail in the "Ask" chapter) is your agreed upon set of norms, behaviors and etiquette for how people want to "be" with each other. Best written by the employees themselves, the WTA is their code of conduct or compact. As shared in the first example about communications and messaging, lead with your purpose statement in the Working Together Agreement.

5. Connect your purpose to your values and make them visible, too. A simple way to make values more apparent is to use them for names of meeting rooms. ("Let's meet in the Integrity Room.") They can be words on your story wall. When you have people gather for a meeting open with a quick round of, "Share one thing you have done this week that relates to our value of transparency" and ask each person to quickly write it in the chat. (Give them a word limit to keep it fast moving.)

6. Create a personality wall that showcases your people. Hire a professional photographer to take photos of each person with an icon representing a favorite hobby or their pet, family member, friend or other meaningful characteristic that represents who they are. In addition to a physical manifestation in the office, make the installation digital by uploading profiles and photos on your intranet page. Create videos of short interviews with each employee and have one of the questions be, "How do you see your work contributing to our overall purpose?"

Engaging ALL employees in a vision discussion is vital to building and achieving purpose.

When the term "strategic planning" is uttered, an image of a handful of leaders heading to a tropical retreat comes to mind. Yet by including all your employees in visioning, you can build a connection and establish "ownership" from the beginning of the change process.

The financial services client mentioned previously, whose employees' commutes would quadruple with the HQ relocation, embraced the idea of an all-employee visioning exercise. We held several workshops at the very beginning of the project – long before a building had been imagined, let alone designed.

Figure #8: Story walls remind employees of the organizational vision

The employees participated in the headline exercise (Exercise #1, shared previously) in small groups. They enjoyed the conversations and had fun with the exercise, but most importantly they were included from the beginning in the discussions about a change that would have a big impact on many of them. Their conversations focused on the future, and they became animated about what that future vision could look like.

The CEO was able to use the headlines (output from the exercise) in conversations with his business leaders and, through a series of conversations, the executive team rewrote their purpose statement. Instead of a top-down/exclusive approach, this became an inclusive approach to crafting a purpose statement.

Goal: **To attract more qualified candidates**

Headcount: **85**

A CEO, whose business was located in a town 45 minutes from the state's largest city, was struggling to find qualified candidates for good positions; he was hoping to attract a younger and more diverse workforce. He recognized that despite the company having been in its location for more than 30 years, it was time to move. The CEO's vision for success was clear in his mind – to create a workplace that was a destination, where people couldn't wait to get to work, and where he would have an abundance of qualified candidates for open positions.

Purpose

The CEO, the leadership team and all employees participated in vision sessions where they discussed what sort of impact they wanted, as individuals, to have in their community and on the world. The result of their creative expressions revealed common themes, which were braided into a succinctly stated vision. The vision, which was also connected to individuals' values and directly tied to sustainability, became the galvanizing purpose for the project: "To responsibly grow our business, our people, and our impact."

Language

There was a lot of confusion about appropriate language to describe new ways of working – the company had been working in large old-style workstations since the 1990s. The C-suite was bombarded with negative articles about "open plan offices." The project team adopted two specific words to describe the new work environment: connected and sustainable. They did not use terms like agile, activity-based or open and were consistent when describing the new working environment. They explained that people would be better connected – it would be a place where it was easier to see each other and have places to talk and collaborate. They described a workplace that was sustainable—they were not using more space than necessary and were making decisions that would result in a highly energy efficient building with a smaller carbon footprint than their current headquarters.

Less

The space program that the company originally put together indicated that they would need 20% more space than they currently occupied. After space use analysis, vision sessions and focus group discussions it was determined they could make do with less than half of their original estimate. Less space did not mean that people were squeezed like sardines in workstations stacked back-to-back. Instead, what it meant was that there were a variety of places that employees could choose to work, ranging from a comfortable lounge chair (9 square feet) to a sit/stand workstation (36 square feet) to an enclosed private focus room with a door (80 square feet). All employees could use these spaces and they moved throughout the day to access the spaces – sharing all spaces as they already shared meeting rooms and lunch rooms. No one "owns" any one seat. And by using less space the company was better able to achieve their vision and create a work environment that allowed people to connect with purpose.

Ask

Inviting employees into conversations from the very first discussion about vision was a key factor in building buy-in and ownership of the result. Employees were thoughtfully and personally invited to contribute. They knew that their voices mattered, and, in fact, they were quite excited to contribute their ideas, many of which positively impacted the final design. Because employees knew they were being listened to from the get-go, they had greater acceptance of the final change.

Net Zero

The building was carefully sited to take advantage of the natural characteristics of the site as well as solar orientation. The building utilizes a carbon sequestering mass-timber framed structure with glulam beams and columns, and some structural steel reinforcements. The high-performance building is designed to exceed existing energy codes by 30%, and has a photovoltaic array on the roof to provide 35-40% of the electricity needed to power the building's electrical and mechanical systems. The additional up-front costs for the improved thermal envelope and photovoltaic array will be offset by significant energy savings that will pay back the initial investment in less than 10 years. It was because of the focus on the first several tenets (purpose, language, less and ask) that it was easier to make decisions regarding up-front costs to obtain a lower-impact building.

Equity

Through anonymous surveys and focus groups we learned that employees felt there were siloes and class distinctions between different departmental groups. The organization talked about equity and its meaning as applied to their hiring practices, professional development and measurement processes, as well as the physical workplace design. For example, instead of large multi-stall gender specific restrooms, single user gender neutral restrooms were designed and built throughout the office.

Time

The CEO, from his very first consideration of the headquarters building, through to occupancy two years later, recognized this was the right time to question how things had always been done relative to work and the workplace. Asked if he wished he had done anything differently he said, "No, nothing." After a slight pause he smiled, "But I'm never going to do it again, because I don't have to." The CEO created his "forever" workplace that will support company employees for decades.

His vision was realized when, only a month after moving into the new offices, people expressed enthusiasm, excitement, and ownership of the resulting change. Importantly, the vision the CEO had for the change – to attract more qualified candidates for openings – wildly exceeded his expectations. He received over 100 applicants for positions where previously he struggled to find ten.

The CEO acknowledged that relocating the company headquarters played a large part in the success of their recent recruiting efforts. Three years after the relocation he said, "We retained 98% of our pre-relocation staff even though there was a lot of fear and apprehension about longer commutes for many of them – their engagement has never been higher."

LANGUAGE

Words matter. Words communicate not only meaning but emotion, they can both unite and divide a group with diverse interests. In the physical workplace, there are many words that mean different things to different people. Then there is jargon, words that can obfuscate meaning.

If you announce to your staff that you will be making physical changes in the office, be prepared for a deluge of *Wall Street Journal* articles about the workplace forwarded to you by employees who are concerned about any change to the status quo. The problem with those *New York Times*, *Wall Street Journal* and *Washington Post* articles they send you is that they conflate all terms relating to "the office" under one big, nasty, negative umbrella: "Open-Plan Workspaces Lower Productivity and Employee Morale"[21] "Open offices are making us all sick"[22] It is important to be very clear and consistent with the words you use to describe workplace change. Reference the "Terminology" sidebar for examples: Look at the terms in the box. Can you see how without an agreed upon, shared meaning the words might cause confusion or misunderstanding?

It is important that there is mutual agreement on the words and concepts related to the proposed change. Once meaning is agreed, the leaders and project team must "stick to the script" to eliminate confusion among stakeholders, otherwise, people may use their own interpretation, or be influenced by headlines they have read. It may easily be the case that the negative headline they are reading is not about the type of change you are introducing. But they do not know that because the terminology and definitions are fuzzy or different than yours.

Word	Possible meaning
Agile	• shared working spaces • a process used in IT • nimble
Flexible	• ability to work when I want (flexible hours) • ability to work where I want (at home, in the office, a third space)
Hot Desking	• unassigned seating; moving from desk to desk with no assigned seat • a free-for-all, people sitting wherever they want • sitting in a certain "neighborhood" and sharing a desk with others in my team/department
Hybrid	• a choice in where I work - sometimes in the office, sometimes at home • working at the office 2 days a week and at home 3 days a week • working at home all the time except 2 times a month
Open Plan	• a sea of desks with no dividers between them • a wide open space with no alternative working spaces (no privacy)
Remote	• working in another geographic location from the primary office • working from home
Shared	• sharing my desk with one other person • not having a desk at all - sharing everything with everyone
Unassigned	• not having a specific place to sit when I go to the office • sharing a desk with other people

The importance of clarifying concepts and using consistent, precise language cannot be overstated. There are not universally accepted definitions for many of these terms, which is why it is critical to make your definition clear. Whatever terms you use, I recommend that the project team publish a language lexicon to ensure there is no misinterpretation of the terms and concepts being used.

A Note About Terminology in the Workplace

Numerous terms are conflated when considering today's work environments: activity-based work, hot desking, hoteling, flex work, open plan and agile working are a few examples. The word "agile" originated from the Information Technology (IT) world and is still a much-used way of completing IT projects. "Agile" made its way into the physical workplace as a way of describing a work environment. When used in this context, "agile working" simply means working when and where you need to in order to do your best work.

It is important to understand the different terms because articles about the office often wrongly lump various types of workspaces into one category. Here's a list of current terms, correctly defined, to describe the physical workplace:

activity-based working (ABW) - this is the concept of choosing a place to work that supports the work you are doing at the moment; e.g., sitting by a window in a lounge chair to write a report for an hour, moving to a stand-up desk to answer emails for 30 minutes, moving to an enclosed meeting room for a brainstorming session, and then stepping into a private focused room to complete a task requiring concentration and deep work.[23]

hot desking, flex work, agile working - these terms have similar meaning: desks are located in "neighborhoods", people are not assigned a specific desk that they "own." Employees may choose a desk to work at within their neighborhood of teammates. However, they can also choose a different place to work away from their neighborhood and are encouraged to move throughout the day if that movement supports their work. (see Activity-based working)

hoteling - desks that are available for drop-in employees or visitors; the hotel desks are reserved ahead of time, similar to a hotel room.

open plan - refers to an office area with low, or no, furniture partitions (panels) between desks; people sit in a common, or "bullpen", area and there are no other choices of different places to sit, such as private rooms or lounge chairs.

How Language Can Impact Understanding of a Change

Below are three examples of how the language tenet can influence how people view a change ("Experience 1", "Experience 2" and "Experience 3"). The team leading the change first agreed to the words and concepts relative to the change and then stuck to their script. This eliminated confusion among stakeholders, including the managers and employees as well as the internal teams involved in the change - such as IT, Facilities Management (FM), Real Estate and Design.

Words matter, not just for their intent, but for how they are interpreted. Workplaces are often overrun with jargon, both relative to the business and to the workplace change and design. So the terms and phrases we use really matter.

EXPERIENCE 1

A financial services company with 300 employees decided they would close two of their offices – one in a large city and one in a suburb about 30 miles from that city – and lease space from a coworking company. They had determined that the utilization of both of their offices was very low – 30% in the case of the suburb and 50% in the larger office. Leasing a coworking space would allow them to save considerable costs on real estate. At first, the new space was being called by the name of the coworking organization – it was a WeWork space.

In early conversations, the team recognized that it was important to let employees know that the space they would be moving to was going to be 100% occupied by only the company's employees. Non-employees or strangers would not be wandering into their offices as you would experience with a typical coworking space.

So, the team started calling the project by the building street address, 27 Lincoln Place, instead of by the coworking company name ("WeWork"). This may seem minor, but it was important because it set the tone for what this move meant – it was a commitment to an office space and was going to be branded as their previous corporate space had been. This gave employees a measure of confidence that this move was not an interim or temporary move or that they would become anonymous workers blended with others in a building.

The president of a bank constructing a new operations center recognized the importance of language and insisted the change management and design teams not use the terms "open office" or "open plan" when discussing the new environment. He was very careful when describing the type of workplace he envisioned – more than 30% of his employees had private offices and they were very concerned about what the new modern office would look like, rightly expecting that there would be fewer private offices in the new building. Employees emailed the president articles about the negative aspects of open plan offices. He was consistent and measured with his responses and language, saying, "This does not describe the workplace we are creating. We are creating an office that is light, bright, allows you to connect with others, and gives you private rooms and choices of where to work." He stayed away from jargon like activity-based, agile, or open plan.

The city of Portland, Maine was planning its vision for the next 30 years. The planning department created a document to reflect the plan and called this document a "comprehensive plan." Maine is a rural state with the highest percentage of non-Hispanic whites in the country. However, in Portland, its largest city, more than 60 different languages are spoken. Portland is a very diverse city.

In 2015, Portland's vision for its future in 2030 was to be a city that is connected, authentic, secure, sustainable, equitable and dynamic.[24] The city planning department created a graphic that showed these primary words and other words that related to the statement. A simpler graphic was then printed on t-shirts, but the six primary words were written in the top languages spoken in Portland: Arabic, English, Portuguese, Spanish, Somali and French. *(image #9)*

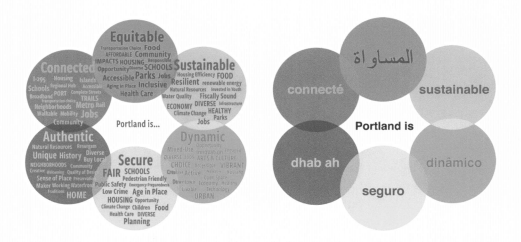

Image #9 – City of Portland, Maine vision statement (left) and t-shirt design (right). The words, clockwise starting at top, are written in Arabic, English, Portuguese, Spanish, Somali, and French. Design credit: City of Portland, Maine

A planning board member wore one of the shirts to run an errand at her neighborhood market. As she was standing in front of the register to buy a soda, she noticed the cashier studying her shirt. He recognized one of the words written in his native language. This interaction led to a moment where the planning board member could explain to the shopkeeper what the city's comprehensive plan was and what Portland was hoping to achieve.

Words matter. They have the power to change both hearts and minds. They can create a sense of belonging. This story also illustrates equity, (which is one of our 7 tenets that we will discuss in a future chapter) because the planning board member wanted to have conversations with people in the community that often were not included. It was an intentional action on her part – and it worked.

Goal: **To create an inspiring space that supports a person with pressing deadlines**

Headcount: **1**

You might be surprised to learn that the 7 PLLANET tenets can apply to a home office. With more people wishing to develop individual workspaces at home, I encourage you to try PLLANET for your home office. A highly successful journalist for an international publication who was also writing a book needed a place to call her own. Jean had been working on her manuscript for a couple of years, in between her newspaper assignments. She was a gifted writer and had high standards for her work. Jean had a room in her house that served as a guest bedroom and as an office. The space was cluttered and visually chaotic. It was perfect for a PLLANET intervention.

Purpose

Jean took time to envision what success would look like when her book was published. This project was deeply meaningful to her and by clarifying a vision for success, it helped motivate her to meet looming deadlines. She wrote her purpose statement on sticky notes and placed them throughout her home – on the bathroom mirror, her computer monitor, and on her bedside table.

Language

The process of carving out a space for one's own use when sharing a space with a partner, children or other family members can feel selfish. Yet, by using language that focused on outcomes, her work, and the process of writing, Jean was able to articulate why she could not share the office with her partner, who was also a writer. You can imagine the delicate nature of defining a workspace when your coworker is also your husband. Choosing words carefully and being considerate of the other's feelings is a skill to use in the workplace and at home.

Less

Less played an important part in this transition from a cluttered workspace to a more organized and sparse office. Jean had a work style where visibility was important – she literally needed to see the tasks and projects in front of her. Recognizing how you personally work and establishing a system to support how you work is critical. An enclosed file cabinet or an electronic catalog system would not be a good fit for how Jean needed to work. To better support her work style, we identified all of the tasks and categories that Jean needed to reference for her newspaper writing and her book writing. We used open-topped magazine bins with labels on each one to capture the notes, memorabilia and other physical aspects of her work. These were lined up on open shelves above her desk and, at a glance, she could easily find what she needed to reference.

Ask

When you are designing a workspace for yourself, ask, "What allows me to do my best work?" Carefully consider all aspects – your dominant hand, where things need to be located to be within easy reach, what you need (quiet, music, a buzz of a coffee shop), your highest energy times throughout the day for certain tasks (and your lowest energy times for other tasks that may require less concentration, focus or creativity), your favorite colors, scents, artwork, lighting, plants, access to natural light, and temperature. You are creating a space custom tailored to you, so get it right.

Net Zero

Jean already had reduced her carbon footprint because she did not commute to a separate office. She considered what modifications could be done within her home to use less energy and had insulating window coverings installed. Jean looked at her own impact and, already a vegetarian, decided that becoming vegan was another step she wanted to take toward reducing her carbon footprint.

Equity

Equity is very important to pay attention to with a home office, especially if you are an employer supporting your people with creating their home working environments. In Jean's case, she was fortunate because internet speed, having space in her home, and having an appropriate background for virtual meetings were not issues. That is not the case for everyone.

82% of white adults in the U.S. report owning a desktop or laptop computer compared to 58% of Blacks and 57% of Latinx. Similarly, 79% of white adults report having broadband internet compared to 66% of Black and 61% of Latinx.[25,26] One's background in a Zoom meeting can convey economic status and, whether we are conscious of it or not, that physical background can impact our judgement of the meeting participant's status and competency.[27]

Time

This was the right time for Jean to claim a space that would support her doing her best work. She shared that the focus on her own needs felt selfish to her at first. Yet, she also said that the process was very rewarding and, although she had identified professionally as a writer for many years, she finally could exclaim with authority, "I am a writer!"

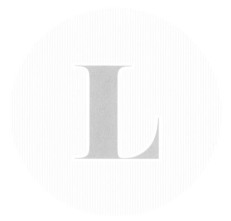

LESS

If you want to transition to a workplace that cares about the planet and our shared futures, a space your employees know is striving to be part of the solution, not part of the problem, you need LESS. Using less does not have to be painful.

The entire commercial office industry is built upon the concept of "more." Office space is quite literally the commodification of space, and when it comes to commercial real estate, every player in the game takes their cut. Real estate brokers make their commission on the sales and leasing of office space – the more space an organization takes in an office building, the higher the broker's commission. Construction is based on a per square footage cost, and architects and interior designers make their living, typically, with a fee based on construction costs or square footage. Everyone from the design professional to the contractor, the real estate agent to the furniture dealer benefits when you take more space.

Yet, commercial buildings are a major contributing factor to global warming. What that means is the carbon that is emitted from the construction of the building and embodied carbon in furniture products that comprise an office, as well as carbon emitted to keep the building operational, are significant contributors to carbon emissions.

People can work in a smaller footprint, so why is it so hard to change our method of determining how much office space we need? Simple. It is because the facility management and real estate professionals making decisions about space are afraid of making a mistake. They don't want to let you down. It is much easier to have more space to grow into – to not be caught short as an organization expands.

Facility professionals approach the daunting task of building a new office from a place of safety and status quo. And who can blame them? They are knowledgeable, experienced and more times than they care to remember, have dealt with people second guessing how the office is being designed. These are the professionals who are best positioned to share how new ways of working can effectively meet organizational needs in fewer square feet. To do that, however, they need to either work for a forward-looking leader who encourages them to challenge the status quo, and invites them to participate in strategy, or they need to have the courage and tenacity to ask their leaders to do things differently. Business leaders who rely on the office planning mathematics of the 1990s show themselves as outdated and left behind.

How it has been done for 30+ years

What I mean by status quo is that facility managers use a calculation of square feet per person based upon how the company is currently operating and then project that number forward, including a contingency for expected growth. This is how we planned offices in the 1990s. Like many habits of three decades ago, it is time to move on. We are relying on outdated tenets for planning office space. The world of work has changed a lot since the 1990s, primarily driven by technology improvements.

Computer monitors of the 1990's were 24" deep, requiring a deep corner worksurface; now flat screens are less than an 1" thick. Desk phones took up 100 square inches; today's phones slip into a pocket. IT servers required a raised floor and large dedicated rooms for equipment; now servers hang on a wall or are in a cloud. Individual private offices were 200 square feet and had a desk in the middle with two guest chairs in front of it; today's meetings can happen virtually or in a more comfortable and casual environment such as two lounge chairs that require less than a total of 20 square feet.

Facility managers and designers often estimate how much space an organization will need on a square footage calculation: For example, 300 employees x 150 SF/employee = 45,000 square feet. This number will then be inflated to include additional space for growth and circulation, areas such as hallways and passageways. The number will also include a lease factor, a charge for common areas of the building such as the lobby, elevator and restrooms.

When each professional engaged in helping calculate how much space you need is benefiting when you take more, what is their motivation to tell you that you need less space? Right. There is none.

The LESS idea has arrived because we are overdue for a new model for working, and the global pandemic has provided findings from a large-scale experiment forced on former workplace occupants. We do not need as much space as we have had. We will save money, too, but that is not the primary driver. Most of the country and indeed the world have just spent a year working from home. The Leesman 2021 survey indicates 48% of people want to continue to work from home 2 to 3 days a week and 37% would be happy working 4 or more days a week at home.[28] These results are consistent across numerous surveys ranging from Global Workplace Analytics[29] to Steelcase (office furniture manufacturer)[30] and McKinsey.[31] To provide a dedicated desk for each employee in an organization in 2021 makes as much sense as giving every customer an assigned shopping cart for when they visit the supermarket; it is wasteful, expensive and requires a large amount of storage space.

Commercial office buildings are responsible for almost 40% of contributing emissions.[32] Energy demand from buildings and construction continues to rise, partly driven by the growth in buildings' floor area. We in the United States like to have space around us; historically, we see size as an indication of status. Our newly constructed houses average 2200 square feet[33] and the average family size is 3.14 [34], leading to an average of 700 sf of living space per person. By comparison, newly constructed houses in the United Kingdom average 826 square feet[35] for 2.37[36] people resulting in 348 square feet per person.

Our desire for expansiveness means the US lags behind many countries when it comes to creating more efficient offices with fewer square feet per person. The average office building in the US requires 150 usable square feet per employee. An office in the UK, on the other hand, averages 100 usable square feet per employee. ("Useable square feet" means the amount of space actually occupied or used, as compared to "leasable square feet" which is the amount you pay for and typically includes a factor to account for shared building space). Using less space in our offices and in our homes is a cultural shift, but one that we need to embrace now to counter climate change.

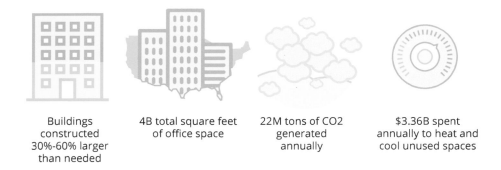

| Buildings constructed 30%-60% larger than needed | 4B total square feet of office space | 22M tons of CO2 generated annually | $3.36B spent annually to heat and cool unused spaces |

Figure #10: Office buildings in the United States before the pandemic.

The Not-So-Big-Office

The negative impact of the old approach is that office spaces are being constructed that are 30% to 60% larger than necessary. With office buildings accounting for approximately 4 billion square feet of real estate in the United States, this is a tremendous amount of wasted space. In a year, unused space in buildings generates 22M tons of CO_2 annually. Also, $3.36 billion is spent on electricity to power, heat and cool spaces that aren't used.[34] Note that these numbers are all statistics before we experienced a global pandemic. (*figure 10*)

I care about this because I see it as a huge opportunity to make a positive difference in climate change by using less space. Taking a page from Sarah Susanka, the residential architect who championed the not-so-big-house movement[38], I call it the "not-so-big-office."

The greenest building we can create is, of course, the one we do not build. But if you must build, build less. We need to combat global warming NOW. Time is running out to ensure our planet does not increase its temperature more than 1.5 degrees Celsius and we can do that by lessening the amount of greenhouse gasses released into the atmosphere. We already have more than enough buildings to support workers and, especially now after the pandemic, most organizations have far more space than they need, especially if they encourage at least some remote working.

We have two external factors that give us the opportunity to use less: changing desires post-pandemic for how people work, and global warming. What the post-pandemic office needs is a radical and immediate shift in how it is visioned, designed, and built.

Planning your office space as it has always been done – using a square footage number per employee – is an old way of thinking and will not pass muster or respond to how people want to work now or how the planet needs us to work going forward. There will be resistance to doing things differently and to questioning the status quo. Resistance to change is normal. Your leadership and unwavering focus on using less will win out.

Smart working post-pandemic means sharing workspaces

Many experiences in our day-to-day living are shared with others: We share shopping carts, bus, plane and train seats, library books, restaurant tables, taxi cabs. We have never expected that these items will be "assigned" just for our use. I go to the supermarket once or twice a week, grab the first cart I find, do my shopping and then return the cart for the next person. I expect that there are many activities in my everyday life that will cause me to share items with others.

There are three things I never share with anyone: my toothbrush, my cell phone, and my bed pillow.

And I also do not share my desk.

It has been this way (assigned desks) since the beginning of most people's professional careers – people show up to work and are "assigned" a desk or workstation. In fact, earning larger office space is a reward and status achievement in many organizations. However, even before COVID-19, workstation utilization rates hovered around 40% to 60%, meaning that workspaces were vacant 60% to 40% of the time. Private offices were empty 77% of the time.[39]

Now with increased remote working, you can expect that these vacancy numbers will be even higher. Surveys show that people still want to come into an office, but that they expect to come in less often because they will choose to do some tasks from home. As recent surveys have consistently shown, the sweet spot for remote working is 2 to 3 days per week.[40]

Given this expectation for lower office occupancy, coupled with the fact that commercial buildings contribute to carbon emissions, now is the time to rethink the idea of an assigned office or assigned desk for each person.

The smart alternative is to create a variety of work and meeting settings that are multi-purpose and can support people with the tasks they need to do, when they do come to the office.

It will be rare that 100% of all employees show up on the same day. But, even if they did, when you have designed the office to support a variety of work and meeting activities, you will find you have plenty of spaces and choices where people can work. For example, desks, lounge chairs, stand-up tables, individual private rooms, or cafes are all viable spaces to work, depending upon the activities being done. As the data shows (*figure #11*) people will be coming to the office to collaborate, connect, meet and socialize with others, rather than to sit at one desk for 8 hours straight.

Size and Status

But how much space does each person really need? The concept of office size equating with an employee's status comes from the Army, where a soldier's rank was reflected in the size of their office. The higher your rank, the larger your office. To this day, office size and ego are tightly intertwined for many. However, there are options to consider when rethinking what types of spaces best support our work. Figures #12 and #13 illustrate one way to rethink private offices.

The 'before' image (*figure 12*) is of a typical attorney's office – a sizeable desk, with binders and boxes covering the floor, the desk and any other available horizontal surface. The two guest chairs are rarely if ever used, because the attorney meets clients in the conference center (who would bring a client into this mess?) The door takes up a valuable 9 square feet of space – and is usually open anyway. A bookcase holds unused binders and dusty awards.

The after image (*figure 13*) is an office that is 50% smaller than the first office yet allows for greater efficiency and improved productivity. There is plenty of uninterrupted work surface area to lay out files and documents, and a total of 24 lineal feet of shelving to hold cardboard banker boxes – allowing for cases that go on and on to be handled seamlessly. (We know that the legal profession is one of the last bastions of paper-heavy work.)

Windows let in natural light and a sliding glass door allows privacy when needed. (The interior windows and door can be sandblasted to allow visual privacy.) Measurable cost savings would be gained on two levels: improved efficiency and productivity for the attorney, and increased job satisfaction for the assistant located on the other side of the glass, who will now get far more natural light in that space.

In addition, the ability to reduce lease costs by up to 50% for private attorney offices adds up to a significant number. Reducing the size of the offices, and making an efficient "cockpit office," would not only save on operating and lease costs but could improve efficiency and productivity.

Top Reasons To Work From Home

67%	**56%**	**54%**	**46%**
Improve work/life balance	Reduce commuting time	Improve focus and productivity	Reduce costs (gas, lunch, etc.)

Top Reasons To Work At The Office

69%	**56%**	**51%**	**46%**
Collaborate face to face with colleagues	Connect face to face with direct reports or supervisor	Socialize with colleagues and maintain relationships	For a change of scenery, to get out of the house and into an office environment

Figure #11: Top reasons to work from home vs work from office

This type of change seems like a no-brainer, yet attorneys may hesitate. Don't give up hope. If you use the PLLANET change process you have a better chance of bringing them on board. A law firm I worked with used this office design with great success for their paralegals and newer attorneys.

The way we have designed and used office space has remained largely unchanged for decades without questioning certain basic assumptions. We could make a good analogy here with the size of cars. When office space was limitless and cheap and the copier a modern marvel of course it got its own room. People also drove large, luxurious Buicks and Cadillacs when gas was 10 cents a gallon. New information and new technologies mean changing sizes.

Now is the time to question embedded assumptions and challenge conventional thinking.

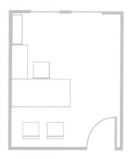

BEFORE: A typical attorney's office is shown in the photo and floor plan. File cabinets are located outside of the office, near the assistant. As a result, often there are piles of papers, boxes, and binders on the floor and at the occupant's feet. The swinging door takes up valuable space and the chairs are seldom used (because who would want a client to see this mess?). The solid wall and door block natural light from penetrating into the space beyond the private office.

DESCRIPTION	BEFORE	AFTER
Size (feet / meters)	14' x 11' / 4.3 x 3.3	8' x 10' / 2.4 x 3
Square Feet / Square Meters	155 sf / x 14.2 sq m	80 sf / 7.2 sq m
Desk area	25 sf / 2.3 sq m	27 sf / 2.5 sq m
Lineal shelving + filing	9 feet / 2.7 m	24 feet / 7.3 m
File storage location	Outside of office near assistant	Inside office near attorney
Door swing (unusable space)	9 sf / .8 sq m	0 sf / 0 sq m
Guest Seating	2	2
Natural light penetration	20% (when door is open)	100% (even when door is closed)

Figure #12 shows a "before" office which was inefficient and did not support how the occupant needed to work.

Rendering: James Reben

AFTER: A redesigned attorney's office is shown in the image and floor plan. File storage is provided on the shelves, located within arm's reach of the desk. Full height sliding glass door and sidelights allow natural light into interior spaces.

PERCENTAGE CHANGE

Office size
reduced 50%

Desk area
increased 8%

Shelving + File
Storage
increased 167%

Natural light
penetration increased
400%

Figure #13 shows a redesigned space that uses less space and better supports this person's work style.

Small shifts = big changes

I attended an early morning boot camp a few years ago, and during an excruciating set of leg lifts, the instructor pointed out that a subtle shift in how I point my toe would exercise a different muscle. I thought, "Well, if that works for my body, I wonder if it will work for my mind…If I shift my thinking about something just one degree, can I experience a wholly different perspective or point of view?" The answer, I learned, is, "yes!" Small shifts can help you create bold change in your workspace.

Efficient use of space can have a big impact on how much office space you require, and small changes can have big collective impact. Two examples of efficient space principles follow about meeting spaces and mail/copy rooms. Taken individually, these may seem like small space-saving gestures. But, when multiplied across many floors, buildings, cities and countries, the impact becomes significant. Anything we can do to use less space will have an eventual bottom-line benefit to the environment, as well as to money saved on overhead.

Meeting Rooms

Let's use a typical meeting room as an example of how a slight shift in perspective can make a big difference. Most conference rooms have a rectangular table in the middle of a room which is surrounded by 8 chairs. If you have enough alternative meeting spaces in your office, then remove the table from one of your standard meeting rooms and leave only six chairs, placed in a circle. Tell people to bring notebooks or clipboards if they want to take handwritten notes. Or, have them bring their iPads or laptops and put them on their lap (after all they are called LAPtops.) This small change can cause a big shift in your culture. How? Watch how people interact when they do not have a large flat horizontal table surface as a physical barrier. See how conversation moves around the circle when there is not a designated "head of the table." Notice how one needs to be present in a meeting when he cannot text or skim iPhone messages by hiding a device under the table.

Designate this room for meetings of six or fewer people – resist the urge to pull more chairs in and cram them in the corners. Try it for three weeks and see what happens – I guarantee you will start to see big shifts in culture - at least while people are working in that room. Some changes to expect may be shorter meetings, more positive interactions with employees and higher energy discussions. You may see that employees like the change. The room could also be 50% smaller than a room with a table in it. So as you plan future meeting spaces, remember that you have a choice in what size is the "right" size.

Image of Typical Meeting Room

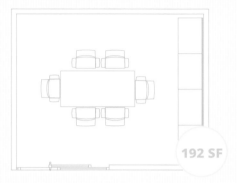

Floor Plan of Typical Meeting Room

192 SF

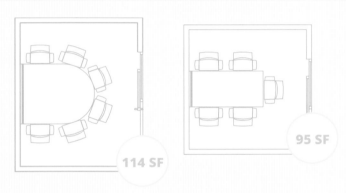

114 SF

95 SF

Floor Plans of Two Proposed Meeting Room Configurations

Meeting Rooms have been designed for an all in-person presence, with a rectangular table in the middle of the room and space on four sides for chairs. An almost-always empty credenza sits at the end of the room underneath a wall-mounted monitor.

We now rely on video conferencing, monitors, cameras, and microphones for meetings, meaning that a room with a table pushed against one wall, with space on three sides for chairs, and a monitor with camera on the wall, provides a better user experience as illustrated in the diagrams.

This room can be 50% to 40% smaller than a room with a table in the center and still accommodate the same number of people as the larger room did.

Figure #14: Diagrams showing how a smaller room can still accommodate a meeting with 5 to 6 people.

116 SF

Image of Typical Mail/Copy Room   Floor Plan of Typical Mail/Copy Room

Rethink the purpose of a copy/mail room, or question if you need one at all. These rooms are often based upon an expectation of multiple daily mailings. The image shows an under-utilized mail room: The supply cabinets have been constructed to hold 3-ring binders, reams of paper and bundles of paperclips that are used far less frequently in a digital world.

Upper storage cabinets are problematic for a large segment of employees to reach because they are so high and the people that need to access them are often short. Because of this the upper shelves remain empty as shown in the photo. Shelves underneath the counter remain empty because they are not needed and are also difficult to access – one has to crouch down to see into the cabinet.

If you do need a mail/copy room, consider redesigning it so it can accommodate required equipment (copy or printer machines) that we use today. Use furniture instead of built-in millwork for storage, which will allow for future flexibility.

Mail/Copy Rooms

Employees' most common request is for a greater number of smaller meeting spaces. Allocating square footage differently can accomplish this. A modular-sized square footage number can be used for construction of copy / mail / storage rooms so those rooms can be used in more versatile ways, responding to the needs of future workers (when, for example, copiers are no longer used, and snail mail is no longer delivered.)

Copy Room
(File Cabinets for Supply Storage)

Locker Room

Game Room

Future Need

If designed in a modular fashion, with no built-in cabinets, we could re-purpose the mail/copy room for a:

• Copy room (Re-Use Existing File Cabinets for storage)
• Meeting Space
• Combined Copy Room and Locker Room - which can encourage more social connection and staff interaction

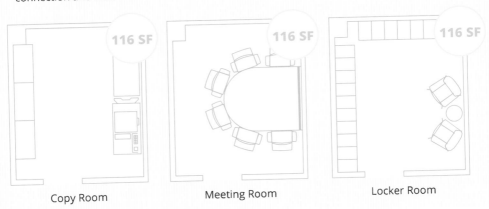

Copy Room   Meeting Room   Locker Room

Figure #15: Showing how the same size room can be more easily repurposed if there are no built-in cabinets

Goal: **To create an equitable workplace for long term growth**

Headcount: **250**

The partners of a 100-member law firm that had been located in a historical building since the 1970s determined it was time to move from the building with drafty windows and a dated interior. Large offices lined the perimeter of the office; the legal staff had no benefit of natural light as the exterior windows were blocked by attorney offices. There were two separate lunchrooms – one for partners and one for everyone else. The firm had strong values: "Experienced. Efficient. Effective." Yet, the office layout had become a barrier to headcount growth and was far from efficient or effective. The physical office and the firm's values did not align.

Purpose

The managing partner was the driver of the vision for the project. He was determined to create a place where all were welcome and where the hierarchical divisions became less entrenched. From the initial conversation about the office with the partners, "efficient and effective", two of the firm's values, also became the oft-repeated planning and design mantra.

Language

Many of the partners were reluctant to consider a changed approach to the office design. The language to describe the project was intentionally focused on "efficient and effective" because those words were woven into the fabric of the firm's DNA. While terms such as "inclusive, equitable, and open" may have resonated with some partners, it was an easier journey to consensus to focus on the pragmatic values upon which the firm was founded.

Less

Less was one of the most visible changes in the design for the new office. An earlier draft of the plan created by the landlord's architect had replicated the former office design: perimeter oversized offices that allowed minimal natural light to the interior spaces. A redesign showed how the new office could accommodate up to 20% more people without increasing the leasable square feet. The layout was efficient and effective.

Ask

Law firms have a reputation for a command-and-control approach with partners making decisions that ripple through the firm. This firm, however, wanted to hear from all staff and invited participation through an anonymous survey and focus groups that included a cross section of positions. The inclusion of all voices led to greater acceptance of the changes. The staff were gaining improvements (natural light and more space) but the attorneys were losing sizable offices. Hearing the staff's comments on working conditions and inequities helped garner acceptance of the changes at the partner level.

Net Zero

Net Zero was not a factor that was specifically considered on this project. However, a more efficient office layout located in a newer building meant that both the operating costs and energy use would be reduced compared to the former dated drafty building.

Equity

There were inequities in the previous office based upon hierarchy. The former location had private offices of up to 350 square feet for partners and attorneys. Paralegals were working in spaces that were 50 square feet or less. Natural light was plentiful for attorneys; everyone else worked in the shadows. The new design used a work area footprint of approximately 110 square feet for every person regardless of title or position within the firm. 110 square foot private offices were designed for efficiency and effectiveness. Workstations for support staff were also about 110 square feet, giving employees plenty of work surface area and storage space. Importantly, all perimeter offices had floor to ceiling glass windows and glass doors, so that the natural light could be enjoyed by everyone; a generous amount of interior glass allowed all areas to be flooded with natural light. Finally, there was one large, vibrant eating area used by all staff – eliminating segregated lunchrooms.

Time

The managing partner was crystal clear that this was the time to make a change that would impact the firm's culture and allow them to grow, expand and recruit talented attorneys in a highly competitive market. As the lease end date on the former space was approaching, he realized that the time to bring his firm into the 21st century was now, and he jumped at the opportunity. His vision and tenacity – it is no small feat to bring law firm partners to agreement on so many radical changes – proved that he was a courageous leader and it was his time to lead.

ASK

Asking is a simple concept, but the activity becomes fraught with concern when it comes to the workplace. As shared previously, leaders go to great lengths to limit input from employees when it comes to change – worrying that they will wish for more than the employer can provide, or it will be impossible to manage their expectations. Yet listening to employees is one of the first things you should do when considering workplace change. How you invite them into a conversation is what "ask" is all about.

Peter Block in *Community: The Structure of Belonging* explains that *how* we invite people into a conversation has a profound impact on the quality of their input and commitment to the outcome.[41] If you receive a personal invitation to a discussion about a specific topic and are told that your input is valuable, how does that compare to an "all staff" email announcing a Town Hall that will be delivered by the CEO?

There is power in face-to-face conversations, even over Microsoft Teams or on Zoom. There is a way to involve everyone in the change process in a way that builds community and employee engagement, and I'm going to show you how in a step-by-step process. This process not only allows you to be inclusive, but also helps people change their behaviors to make a transformation to new ways of working.

"Ask" is one of the most important steps of PLLANET because when you invite people to a conversation about change in an intentional and inclusive manner, you can build lasting community and connection.

A CEO noticed his employees always eating at their desks and he wanted to find a way to discourage that habit and have his people take real breaks from work during the day. He said, "Let's build a cool lunchroom with a ping pong table, Wii games, free sodas, and comfortable booths." His "why" for the change – what he was hoping to achieve – was to get his employees to stop eating at their desks. Thousands of dollars were invested to give the lunchroom a major facelift.

Two months after the change, the CEO commented that people were still eating lunch at their desks. When asked where he typically ate his lunch his response was, "Oh, my desk, of course." The CEO's goal for the change was not met. What needed to happen to transform employee behavior was not clear; the "build it and they will come" approach was not working.

Once the CEO recognized that he and his senior colleagues needed to be visible in the lunchroom, he changed his behavior. He recognized that his actions gave permission (or not) to his employees. Once staff saw leaders using the lunchroom regularly, they recognized that they had permission to use the space and step away from their desks for a legitimate break during the day.

The CEO may have been more successful sooner if he had invited employees into a discussion about habits, breaks, what they really would want in a lunchroom, and what was driving them to eat at their desk every day. By having a listening session and gathering input from his employees, he might have learned that more modest improvements would suffice to update the lunchroom.

The act of listening – inviting people to a discussion with the sole purpose of hearing what is on their minds – can go a long way to alleviating stress in the workplace. As I've said before, our workplaces are a critical component of our wellbeing and have a ripple effect on our families, communities and societies.

The new community of work

Our life expectancy is in the longest sustained decline in a century, not seen in the United State since the four years from 1915 through 1918 which included World War I and a flu pandemic that killed 675,000 people. Deaths due to suicide and drug overdoses continue to rise at alarming rates.[42] *(Figure 16)*

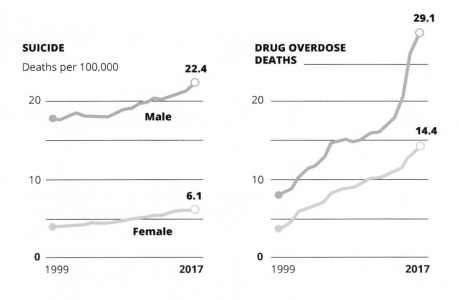

SUICIDE

Deaths per 100,000   **22.4**

20

Male

10

6.1

Female

0

1999   **2017**

DRUG OVERDOSE
DEATHS _____

29.1

20

14.4

10

0

1999   **2017**

Source: Centers for Disease Control and Prevention   The Washington Post

Figure 16: Suicide and drug overdose deaths climb at an alarming rate.

Before COVID-19, people were spending more time at work, leaving less time for community involvement and volunteerism.[43] The office had become many people's community. Business leaders were also serving as community leaders at work, and so had the power to make positive change for many people. But it often required doing things outside of their comfort zone or counter to how things were being done in organizations.

Would you be willing to get uncomfortable if doing so could have a positive impact on life expectancy? How much are you willing to stretch yourself to introduce a method that could save your organization time and money, while also creating authentic connections between employees? How would it feel to have your colleagues look forward to attending one of your meetings? How would you feel if, because of something you do differently, a depressed or isolated employee is lifted and feels less alone in the world? Taking measures to address these authentic reasons can have productivity and financial benefits as well – directly impacting your bottom line.

The Current State: Reactive and Closed

Most physical workplace change happens because of reaction. For example: A department is adding (or letting go) staff and the space needs to align with the business changes. This change is typically conveyed via the CFO or COO to the facility manager. Speed and budget are priorities. The facility group talks to business leaders to see what they want/need, interfaces with an architecture and design team to lay out the floor plan, then has meeting after meeting after meeting as the plans are scrutinized, second-guessed, revised, and finally approved. Typically, the approved plans are second-guessed again when under construction, which leads to last minute changes (known as change-orders in the construction world – invariably increasing costs). These change orders stress out your facility people because they impact both the budget and the deadline.

The people directly impacted by the change – the employees themselves – are not always part of the conversation – and for good reason according to your facility and real estate people. Facilities staff know how fearful employees will be about any change; talking to them about it might promote even more anxiety and then, who will manage their expectations? Plus, talking to employees typically adds more time to a project that already has a tight timeline. It is wise to minimize the number of people we talk to when considering a workplace change…. isn't it?

Although facility management departments have implemented change in a similar way for decades, there is a different way. You can save time by using a specific facilitation method where all voices are heard, and authentic connections are created among participants. This process leads to the work community flourishing and can save time on second-guessed changes during construction.

A Better Mode: Proactive and Open

This alternative method is a tightly facilitated discussion where all voices are invited into a conversation. Technology called Mentimeter[44] or MeetingSift[45] allows this type of discussion to be facilitated in an efficient manner. The result is a more interactive engagement with participants than simply issuing an anonymous survey to everyone, or to delivering a one-way Town Hall monologue. When you use this type of meeting facilitation technology (and it can be used in-person or in a virtual meeting like Zoom or Teams), everyone shares their thoughts by typing comments into a device. Their thoughts are conveyed in real time and are anonymous. The section below illustrates all of the steps and how the method is intentionally designed to invite all voices into the conversation.

Scenario for "Ask"

A department within an automobile manufacturing plant wants to make improvements to its space because of problems with attraction and retention. The business leader has indicated that in recent exit interviews, employees have expressed unhappiness with slow responsiveness to IT issues, not having enough meeting spaces, and lack of areas to concentrate. There are 290 current employees, and the business unit has 15 open positions they are hoping to fill within the next seven months. A decision has been made to invest money into upgrading the space to respond to the above concerns.

Kick-Off Meeting

Designate a facilitator – it could be the business leader or someone else in the company who is a neutral party and respected facilitator. (As you know, not all leaders are great facilitators, so don't let this fall to one of the business leaders as a default. Plus, if the business leader doesn't have to facilitate, then he/she is freed up to participate in the conversation.) Organize a 45-minute meeting with the CFO/COO, designated leaders of IT and HR (or other groups depending upon your organization), the impacted business leader and his Directors/ VPs. Schedule the meeting for no more and no less than 45 minutes. Let the participants know that this will be an interactive session and they will need to bring their phone, iPad or another device to the meeting.

Start the meeting on time. Open the meeting by telling the group that the meeting will be facilitated in a different manner than typically is done (if this is, in fact, a different way than you typically run a meeting). If you are nervous about it, tell the group; let them know that you are trying something new and appreciate their patience and open-mindedness with this meeting. Let them know that your goals with the meeting are to 1) end on time, 2) ensure everyone participates in the discussion, and 3) to have people talk with a different person about each question. This last point is important; let them know ahead of time that they need to move around the room (alternatively, use breakout rooms on your virtual meeting platform) to talk with others when directed.

Give them a brief (5-7 minute) overview of your understanding of the project. In this example you would use the description in the opening scenario, perhaps adding known challenges – that the space will be renovated while it is occupied, or other important considerations.

Three Questions

Ask each participant to speak with the person next to him or her and answer this question, "What is your ideal outcome for this project?" (Or, phrased a different way, "What does success look like for you on this project?") Set your phone timer for two minutes and tell them they are to only converse one-on-one with the person next to them. If you are using virtual breakout rooms, you can set the rooms to automatically place two people in each room and set the timer to close the rooms after two minutes.

After the time is up, ask them to remember what they spoke about, but not to say anything. Have them use their phones to log into the online meeting platform you chose. (Mentimeter or MeetingSift are two platforms. You, as facilitator, will need your laptop connected to a monitor and will need WiFi. I suggest a trial run with family members or friends beforehand – play around with the online platform a bit to be more comfortable when you are conducting the kick-off meeting.)

Meeting attendees enter the sentence/phrases/words that capture highlights of their discussions into their devices. The comments will show up on the screen as they are entered. (*figure 17*) Think of this as a very efficient flip chart process – you are using technology instead of markers and a flip chart, and you don't have the added time of people stating out loud what they talked about. Also, being anonymous tends to raise the level of frankness and openness of the responses.

Figure #17 – Example of Mentimeter output

Review the comments on the screen together. Don't spend more than a couple minutes looking at the list on the screen. The best you can, keep things moving so no one person dominates the airwaves with extraneous comments.

Then, ask them to talk with a different person for two minutes and answer this question, "At this point in time, what is the number one business priority from your point of view?" Same scenario – you set your timer, they chat with a partner, then enter highlights of their discussion into their device. Review the comments quickly – spending only 1-2 minutes. Examples that they might raise include, "recruiting and retaining great talent," "improving the productivity of our people," "improving cross-departmental relationships," or, "improving our sustainability performance."

For the third question, have them pair with a different person: "What are the concerns you have with this project/initiative?" They talk with their partner for two minutes, then input their words into the device. Review the comments on the screen and chat for a couple minutes about the concerns that have been raised.

At this point you will be about 25 minutes into the meeting with 20 minutes to go. Ask the attendees to write as many questions that they may have regarding the project. They can input all of the questions into your online meeting platform. Review them together on the screen, answering quickly what you can in the moment and acknowledging that some of the questions will need further research to answer (for example, specifics on schedules, budgets, amount of disruption, etc.)

Inviting All Voices

Pause and tell the group that this method you have been using in the meeting is a method you would like to use with the employees who will be impacted by the workplace change. You will conduct a tightly facilitated workshop, with the online platform, and will spend no more than 45 minutes with the employees, asking them three or four pre-determined questions and having them talk one-on-one for two minutes with a different partner for each question. (This may mean you need to do several sessions – but, if space allows, this method can be successfully used with 100+ employees at one time and with even more when facilitated virtually.)

The timing of the employee workshop is important. It should occur very early in the planning process. Ideally, it occurs after the visioning and purpose discussion (reference the "purpose" chapter), and before any plans have been drawn or significant decisions made. The value of collecting input, opinions and thoughts from employees will benefit you in several ways:

1. opportunities to exercise empathy and build connections by listening to partners in conversation

2. people know their voices have been heard on topics that matter to them

3. creative insights and ideas from the people who will be most impacted by the change (some of the best recommendations I have heard to improve spaces and processes have come from these early listening sessions)

4. efficient expectation management – often employees are not invited into discussions because of concerns about "managing expectations." When you use this method, people are heard, you can consider their input, but you are not put in a place of promising specific outcomes

Facilities Management and Real Estate Partnering with HR

HR professionals often facilitate employee discussions and workshops. If the FM (Facilities Management) and RE (Real Estate) leaders collaborate with the HR leader, then this method can provide yet another opportunity to build cross-departmental connections and awareness, creating a positive workplace experience for all employees.

Unfortunately, inviting the voices of all employees is not typically done by the real estate or facility manager leader. However, employee ownership of the conversation about their workspace leads to their investment in it. Employees will fear change whether you talk to them or not; conversations accelerate acceptance of change and buy-in of the outcome. Talking about potential change will alleviate some of their concerns, and if you encourage one-on-one conversations, can also build connections between people. I used to facilitate small group discussions with 5-6 people, but after reading Susan Cain's *Quiet: The Power of Introverts in A World That Can't Stop Talking*, I realized that even in a group of five, there may be people who are not comfortable participating.[46] I much prefer the heightened participation, engagement, and connection I see when people talk one-on-one in workshops.

What to Do With Meeting Output

Using this facilitation method from the beginning of a project – first with the leadership team and then with groups of employees – brings everyone along on the change journey. Of course, there are questions or things employees may hope for that won't be realized, but at least they know their voices were heard.

As you continue with the project, issue updates to all staff that show how employee input is being considered or implemented. Don't be afraid to tell them what you couldn't do (due to budget or other constraints) and acknowledge great ideas that you are able to implement. The word clouds and responses that are generated from the meeting facilitation platform can be shared on a company intranet, sent digitally in an email newsletter, or printed out on large sheets of paper and taped to the wall. Reminding people that they were involved from the beginning and that their voices matter, is a way to show them that this is an inclusive process and that the result will be better because of their involvement.

Positive Results

When you provide opportunities for employee input, initial anxiety and trepidation about change will turn to excitement and anticipation. When you combine technology to support an efficient meeting along with one-on-one discussions, you will also see people engage and connect in ways that can be surprising and rewarding. When you have people connect with a different person – even for a couple of minutes – empathy and connection increase, which leads to a stronger community.

The opportunity you have in your role is to lead your organization into a different way of doing things by confidently engaging leaders and employees in the change process through facilitated conversations.

With people spending more time than ever working, you can build true community at work and even turn the tide on the life expectancy in the U.S. Are you willing to try something different?

Several years ago, I fell in love with spinning, also known as indoor cycling. Sessions with a specific instructor, Carolyn, were more enjoyable than others. One day it dawned on me why. Carolyn uses techniques that are equally important in skillful facilitation.

HIGH ENERGY:

Carolyn begins every class with high energy – and she sustains that energy to the end. A skillful facilitator must have a high level of energy to raise the energy of the participants.

SET INTENTION:

Carolyn asks us to close our eyes and set our intention for our ride before it starts – establishing our own mantra. Beginning a session with a check-in and asking participants to think about what they'd like for an outcome brings focus to the task at hand.

FOCUS ON THE PARTICIPANTS:

Carolyn constantly checks the pulse of the room, reminding us the tempo, (1, 2, 1, 2) and ensuring we are keeping up. A skillful facilitator regularly reads the room to see if someone is checked out or struggling with a concept.

CONNECT PARTICIPANTS TO EACH OTHER:

Carolyn invites us, when our energy might be waning, to emanate energy to help each other. This technique is key to establishing an atmosphere of support and camaraderie.

Inviting participants to take the focus off themselves and to instead turn it on someone else allows for stronger interpersonal connections.

BE CONSISTENT AND CLEAR:

Carolyn uses the same language in each class to give us instructions. Whether it is, "1/4 turn to the left" or "two whole turns to the right" she uses phrases that are simple, direct, and clear. Whether you are asking participants to break into small groups or to finish a task in three minutes, being specific, clear and consistent makes it easier for them to focus on their discussions and not worry about the process.

These tips can be kept in mind for any meeting you are facilitating and are especially helpful when doing the "Three Questions" discussions shared previously.

How to Plan Your Workplace for The Future During a Pandemic

Creating a mudroom and creating an office may seem like two widely different activities. But I realized recently that both can benefit from focusing on the long view. I stood in the kitchen doorway, admiring the mudroom we are building. "It seems awfully big," my husband said. "It might be big for us, Pete, but this will serve the next family that grows up in this house."

We live in a house that my father, an architect and engineer, designed in the 1960's. My brother, sister and I grew up here and we never had a mudroom. My husband and I raised our own three children here, sans mudroom. I remember peeling layers of cold wet clothes off icy little legs and then laying snow pants to dry on the furnace in the basement. We've had many a melted snow boot and scorched knit hat to prove it.

A mudroom is a necessity in Maine, where we have long frigid winters that turn into muddy cold springs, bringing dirt, salt, sand, and mud into the house. It is the chamber between inside and outside where one dons warm clothing and boots, drops backpacks and lunch pails, hangs the dog leash and car keys.

And, yes, two families have survived living in this lovely mid-century house without a mudroom. Yet, I knew the house deserved one and was elated when finally, after studying the floor plan for literally decades, I figured out how we could create a mudroom without building an addition.

Our new mudroom will have hooks for enough coats to cloak a large family, a closet for household supplies and a vacuum, a bench that can seat 3 people, a radiant-heated floor to dry wet boots, and a small bathroom right inside the door. We are designing a space that will serve a larger family, not two almost-empty-nesters. We are designing for the future, not for how we live now.

The following thought struck me as I reflected upon what organizations are wrestling with regarding work, workplaces, workforces, and COVID-19. Can an organization envision its future and create a place that will support how it may work in 10 years? How? Here are three questions to get started, and then recommendations to dive deeper.

1. What do you know about the people you wish to attract and retain in your organization? What drives them and what are their values?

If you are interested in recruitment and retention, then consider that connection to purpose is not only important to many employees, but is also an intrinsic human motivator.[47] Flexibility in when and where to work is highly desired by employees. Remote job posts rose 357% in one year between May 2020 and May 2021.[48]

2. What do you know about your work environment and how it was serving your employees before COVID-19? As stated previously, pre-pandemic workplaces were often empty, and people were distracted by noise and interruptions. What else wasn't working so well in your office – what was the equivalent to your "scorched hat on the furnace"? The best way to find out, of course, is to ask your employees directly what aspects of the office hindered them from doing their best work.

3. What do you know about technology and the nature of work, and workflow processes that support your organization? Are there embedded assumptions about how work has always been done that could be challenged?

Technology is constantly evolving and people resist changes, especially work process changes and technology improvements. Many work processes are based on legacy; status quo is comfortable.

Using the 45-minute meeting format shared earlier, and building upon your answers to the questions above, consider pertinent questions for your own organization and then dive deeper by engaging employees in conversations – not just issuing another survey – to hear their responses.

Have a listening session using the tailored facilitation method shared previously and pay attention to the feedback. (For virtual gatherings use Teams or Zoom breakout rooms to support the one-on-one conversations described in the method. You can still use MeetingSift or Mentimeter for reporting out.) After you have determined your vision and purpose, take your employees' input and brainstorm what the future world of work could look like for your organization. Consider:

- What are we doing that we should stop doing?
- What are we doing that we could be doing differently?
- What are our beliefs and values and how are they connected to our work?
- What are the barriers to change and what can we do to overcome them?
- Where is the resistance and how can we move forward?
- What can we do to delight our employees?
- What is our biggest fear with a proposed change?
- How can we improve our employees' work experience by allowing for more choice and flexibility?
- Are there decisions we can make that will positively impact climate change?
- Are there behaviors we can change that will reduce our carbon footprint?

No one has a crystal ball, but we know certain facts about humans, about work, and about our world. When we pull these together and include others in discussions about what matters most to them, we can design for the future – the future of where we hope to go, not the past of where we have been or back to something called "normal." We can improve upon work processes, engage employees by inspiring them with value-driven work, and achieve great things – in a way that will positively impact profit, people, and the planet.

Using "ASK" to Build A Strong Work Community

Pious Ali is a City Councilor who is a highly respected public servant and a role model for building community. Ali's professional life has been built around relationships that strengthen communities. His vision of "community" is answering the question, "What is the common good for all of us?" Ali told me that whatever the issue or initiative he is working on, people get attracted to it for a specific benefit – for either themselves personally or the people around them. People are investing into this "thing" (idea/initiative) so they can get some benefit that will come out of it.

When considering a conversation between employer and employee, Ali's approach of identifying a shared connection to the proposed change and exploring how both can benefit is a template for success.

For example, Ali has done a lot of work in the public school system to ensure the voices of under-represented parents are included. When he approaches someone new, he will say, "I know you have a child in the schools, and I have a child in the schools, but the schools do not engage us. Would you like to work with me to create a greater opportunity for engagement of parents and the schools?" By sharing his connection to the initiative, and identifying the other person's possible interest, he creates an invitation to engage in a conversation which will lead to a mutual benefit to the individual and to the community at large. He shared, "I don't look at what benefit I get personally, but rather the benefit that collectively we gain: What is the benefit to their macro community and to the community at large?"[49] Ali believes that we need to create intentional connections to build a relationship – and, I would add that is especially true at work. We need to be intentional and not leave things to chance (waiting for those serendipitous moments to occur around the water cooler, for example) in order to build stronger ties to each other.

Technology can help us build those connections with each other, and someone who has brilliantly used social media to create a robust community is Mike Doehla, founder of Stronger U. Stronger U is a life-changing nutrition program that recognizes the power of community. Doehla set out with an intention to create a community, to build a "hive mind." He states, "The biggest missing piece in many nutritional efforts is community. Everyone is lonely and I wanted to put people together with coaches and clients helping each other make better choices and build habits – that community makes the entire thing stronger."[50] Stronger U has 70 coaches and 12 remote fulltime employees working from coast to coast. Doehla began with 43 people – mostly friends and family – in April, 2015. That community grew to 1000 in 2016 and now more than 40,000 are engaged in the Stronger U online community. People share their wins and successes, as well as challenges. They ask questions, and most importantly, they know they have an online community to tap into to augment their understanding and knowledge of nutrition.

Ali and Doehla are just two examples of community builders. There are most likely many in your own community that have lessons to share. The action of "ask" can lead to a stronger and more connected work community. One effective method to build that community is the Working Together Agreement.

The process of inviting people – asking them with intention – to a discussion about how they want to "be" with each other can achieve two things: 1) people build empathy and relationships, and 2) their collective work can result in a very useful business document – a "Working Together Agreement."

Working Together Agreement

If, as the leader of your organization, you choose to focus your organization's culture on being environmentally minded, then decisions that call for a minor inconvenience become easier for the group to adapt to when people have been invited into a conversation to codify certain practices. Within medium to large organizations, staff are constantly interacting with a large number of people, many of whom are only casual acquaintances. In these interactions, everyone is trying to coordinate with one another without knowing much about these other people. Once social norms become established, they are reinforced by everyone. This is often referred to as the "culture" of a workplace. In these kinds of settings, a committed group of individuals can effectively change the culture of an entire organization.

The Working Together Agreement process is inclusive and uses the same 45-minute format that the "ask" process uses. People are paired with one partner and are asked two questions: 1) what allows you to have a productive day wherever you are working and 2) what guideline or "norm" can you come up with that would help your partner have that productive day?

This exercise uses empathy and listening to build connections. Because the partner needs to write a norm that helps the other person, it requires him/her to listen carefully. The large group comes back together and the participants report out their suggested norms using the online facilitation platform (Mentimeter, MeetingSift or another program).

All of the suggestions are reviewed by one or two people who align/combine similar ideas and place all suggestions into an anonymous survey. The survey is issued to all employees, and they rate how effective the guideline would be on a scale of 1 to 5 (1 = terrible idea!; 5 = great idea!).

The resulting top-rated guidelines are put into the Working Together Agreement. This is issued as an electronic document for people to sign their commitment to try out the guidelines for several weeks. After 6 to 8 weeks, a pulse survey is issued to check in on how the norms are working, and if any tweaks are required. If people are physically in an office, it can also be printed on a large board, and hung in a highly visible location (lunchroom is usually good). Ask people to sign their names to the Agreement. The act of signing, although not a legal, binding act, does show a commitment and intention to following the norms.

This process creates buy-in, accountability and responsibility for an individual's actions. And, because it was a co-created document, the hard job of policing people's behavior does not fall to any one individual. Instead, people are more likely to hold one another and themselves accountable.

Examples of Working Together Agreement guidelines include:

- We believe that health and wellness are important and so we encourage people to move throughout the day and get outside.

- We have a safe environment for constructive and supportive criticism and a culture that supports giving uncomfortable feedback so that little things do not escalate into major annoyances.

- We end meetings seven minutes before the scheduled time to allow time to shift to our next activity.

- We question if a meeting is the best way to achieve a desired result and choose an alternative method if a meeting can be avoided.

- When in the physical office, we use a moderate voice to be respectful of our colleagues.

- When in a virtual meeting, unless there are extenuating circumstances we keep our videos on.

- We encourage walking, biking and public transportation if one needs to come to the office.

These are just a few examples – the norms can be specific, relating to meeting etiquette and keeping spaces clutter-free. They also can be more philosophical and align to the organization's values and purpose. I've even seen the Working Together Agreement guidelines express a fun spirit such as, "We believe in Taco Tuesdays."

The process of asking all employees and being inclusive is as important – if not more important – than the resulting document. You will also find great value in the resulting Working Together Agreement document. It is especially helpful when onboarding staff. New employees express gratitude that the "how" of a place is expressed relatively quickly – a process that normally might take six or more months for them to learn.

Goal: **Accommodate expanding and shrinking headcounts in a shifting industry**

Headcount: **1200**

A media agency experienced periodic expansion, bringing on freelancers as their varied work demanded, season by season. They were challenged to accommodate the ups and downs of headcount throughout the year, and ensure their people felt productive, connected, and engaged. They also projected a 4% full time employee (FTE) growth per year for the next five years.

Purpose

The agency had a clearly articulated purpose; they lived their values through how they approached everything. With their clients, with their work, and with their own people, their core strategic philosophy was disrupting the status quo.

Language

The agency recognized that transitioning to unassigned seating, known as agile working, would give them the most flexibility to support changing head counts. The leaders realized that the words they used to describe the new environment mattered. People had worked at assigned desks since the beginning of their careers and a change to sharing desks with each other was a major disruption – even if that word was their core philosophy!

They used the term "activity-based working", and asked people to consider the varied activities they did throughout a day and where those tasks could be best completed. Some tasks required sitting at a desk in front of large monitors. Others required sitting in an enclosed quiet place with no distractions, which could be done in a private focus room in the office, or completed remotely, at home. Yet other tasks required brainstorming with colleagues in a meeting room or required more dynamic settings that included interactive media.

By focusing on the activities that needed to be completed, and then creating workspaces that supported a variety of activities, the agency was able to shift attention from sharing a single desk ("my" desk) to sharing a myriad of work spots throughout the office, including meeting rooms, focus rooms, lounge chairs, social spaces, sit/stand desks, window seats and desks ("our" work spots).

Less

The change to activity-based working allowed the agency to make wiser use of its real estate. They had conducted a utilization study (how often desks and meeting rooms were used, or occupied, during an average time of the year) and determined that desks were not occupied 45% of the time on average. They knew that, if they added a variety of work setting options to their space, they could make more efficient use of their office. Rather than move or reduce their office size, however, they extended their lease seven years. With activity-based working the office would accommodate their 4% year over year head count growth for many years to come.

Ask

The agency encouraged people to make an inventory of their typical activities as part of the transition to activity-based working. They had employees participate in workshops to talk about what allowed them to have a productive day at work, and to discuss what types of spaces would best support those activities. By inviting employees into meaningful conversations about how they worked best, and what types of activities they did, they were able to co-create their ideal work environment. Because employees were involved in these discussions, they had greater buy-in of the resulting workplace design.

Net Zero

The agency leaders were serious about how they could impact the environment. Their corporate responsibility environmental goal stated, "We take action to increase efficiency and reduce waste in ways that address environmental priorities…We reduce our office space footprint and use the space we lease more efficiently to reduce costs and environmental impacts, while also cultivating a culture of collaboration and creativity." In addition to making better use of real estate, they stopped purchasing new furniture and instead used furniture-as-a-service. Their internal "green team" doubled down on behaviors to reduce paper, eliminate single use plastics, encourage public transportation and biking, and increase remote days to reduce overall commuting. The agency made a significant commitment to reduce air travel by 85% through use of immersive technology for client presentations and remote participation in conferences.

Equity

The agency recognized that people of color were less likely to want to return to the office.[53] The leaders wanted to make a positive difference for all of their staff and decided to adopt Results Only Work Environment (ROWE) which emphasizes autonomy and outcomes instead of insisting on visible presence in the office.

Time

The CEO used the disruption of Covid as an opportunity to reimagine how work could be done better. She utilized lessons learned from the remote working experiment to create a welcoming, inclusive, and modern way of working. This approach extended to how people were managed. She shared that before Covid, managing was akin to "onsite parenting." It was assumed people were being managed if both managers and employees were in the office together. Remote working revealed the need to ensure managers were trained and upskilled to support and coach their people, no matter where employees were working.

NET ZERO

We have no choice. If we don't start working towards net zero carbon emissions and slowing the rate at which we dump our waste into landfills, our time on Planet Earth will run out. To tackle this problem, the work of every single person is needed; as a business leader, you have the unique opportunity to make a substantially bigger difference than some. The world needs you to make better choices. The good news is those better choices may also inspire your employees, build community, and save you money.

As stated previously, commercial buildings contribute substantially to carbon emissions. This negative impact on the environment is due to 1) the fabrication of construction materials and 2) the everyday operations of commercial buildings. Concrete and steel are created in ways that are harmful to climate change. Major office furniture manufacturers (Steelcase, Herman Miller, and HumanScale, among others) have focused on sustainably sourced components for years. However, the positive changes are far outweighed by the negative reality: millions of tons of furniture in the U.S. alone ends up in a landfill. Every year.

Office Furniture

Discarding used office furniture is one of the most difficult tasks for any office manager dealing with a renovation or relocation. There are only so many non-profits that can use your 14-foot long, football-shaped fake wood table. Office furniture becomes obsolete, chairs break, and workstation panel wall heights go in and out of fashion as often as hem lengths and tie widths.

Furniture waste in the United States more than doubled between 1980 and 2018, growing from 5 million to 12.4 million tons. In 2018 only 3% (40,000 tons) was recycled. 19.5% was combusted and 80% went to landfill.[53]

Office Construction

While the industry researches environment-friendly construction materials and adopts greener ways of building, the greenest solution by far is to stop building and make existing office space and furnishings last longer.

When an office space can be designed for maximum flexibility, it can greatly reduce the need for constant renovations. In commercial office planning and design, a renovation to office space is called a "tenant fit-up." Unlike a house, where a new owner usually adapts his or her ways of living to the existing house plan with minor cosmetic improvements such as paint or carpet, a new occupant of a commercial office space tends to plan major renovations.

Remote and Hybrid Work

In March 2020, the world closed down and every office from government to the private sector sent workers home. The impact that a global shut down had on commuting was dramatic: suddenly thousands of cars were off the road. In the United States, transportation accounts for 29% of greenhouse gas emissions.[54] In the early days of the pandemic, we saw air quality improving in large cities because there were far fewer cars on the road. From the middle of March 2020 to the middle of September 2020, commuting time was reduced by 62.4 million hours per day with aggregate time savings of over 9 billion hours. (*figure 18*) [55]

Remote working will most likely keep increasing into the next decade. It is predicted that 36.2 million workers (22% of Americans) will be working remotely by 2025. This is an 87% increase from pre-pandemic levels. Global Workplace Analytics estimates that 56% of workers or 75 million employees could work form home if their employers allowed it.[56]

We learned through the pandemic that many jobs can be done when working from home, and given a choice, employees overwhelmingly want a hybrid working option. One study indicated that 72% prefer hybrid, 12% want to always be in the office and 13% want to always work from home.[57]As a result, organizations and industries are reducing the amount of real estate they occupy while increasing their support of remote working for employees. The purpose, and size, of our offices are up for review, as are our ways of working. The time to question embedded assumptions is now.

From March 2022 to September 2022

9B+ hrs

Daily Aggregate
Time Savings

62.4M hrs

Daily Commute
Time Reduced

Figure #18: Daily commuting during the pandemic

There are numerous ways to create a workspace that treads lightly on the planet. These include encouraging:

- Remote working
- Carpooling
- No paper/printing
- Public transportation
- Use of solar/alternative energy
- Coworking/sharing office space
- Hybrid working

- Biking + walking
- Composting
- Recycling + repurposing furniture
- Design of an energy efficient building envelope
- Not-so-big space
- Hub + Spoke / Satellite Office

When you commit to putting the planet at the center of your purpose conversation regarding the workplace, you will uncover more ways to reduce your organization's impact on the climate. Inviting your staff to contribute their ideas will lead to innovations and new ways of working that may be unexpected and novel – and, best of all, have a greater chance of being embraced by employees because they were part of the conversation from the beginning of the process.

Asoebi and Results Only Work Environments (ROWE)

Something struck me as my family discussed my niece's upcoming wedding, a long-awaited affair that had been postponed due to the pandemic: My niece and her fiancé are including a custom of Asoebi as part of their celebration. As explained by my niece, "Asoebi is a uniform dress that is traditionally worn in West African cultures as an indicator of solidarity during ceremonies and festive periods. The word aso means cloth and ebi means family, so Asoebi can be translated as family cloth...this is a lovely representation of our two families becoming one, and we are inviting anyone attending the wedding to participate."

I love the tradition and as I was musing about what my family and I might design with the cloth to wear at the reception, I couldn't help but think about workers, the workplace, and what they are asking for now, compared to what many employers are ready to provide. Employees want a custom-fit work experience. Many have been able to adjust their work settings and surroundings to what fits them while working remotely. Employers, before COVID, provided a one-size-fits-all work experience, like a poncho. People trudged into an office in a world of sameness: wearing their khakis and white shirts, they sat at a desk in a row of other desks, in front of a computer in a bland open office. Either is an extreme example, but there is an opportunity to find a middle ground.

Using asoebi as a metaphor, an organization can provide yards of fabric (space, equipment, time, and choice of place) and invite their people to consider what best fits their way of working. This exercise is not done in a vacuum without regard to the company and team needs. It is accomplished through conversation, thought, inquiry and listening.

An asoebi process is not as expensive (cost per employee) as a custom-tailored suit, nor is it as quick and easy as cutting a hole in a garbage bag and throwing it over people's heads. An asoebi approach to work already exists and has been tested with positive results since 2004. It is called "ROWE" or "Results Only Work Environment" and was developed by two Best Buy employees.

In 2004, Best Buy was challenged with retaining their talent. Best Buy's corporate HQ, located in Minneapolis/St Paul, had competition from several other well-known companies in that area and their people were job hopping. You may be seeing the same thing happen around you now. We've heard the stories of the great resignation – people are on the move, looking for work that fits them.

Two employees at Best Buy, Cali Ressler who designed work-life programs for employees and Jody Thompson, a change manager for the company, recognized that what people really wanted was autonomy. Not flexibility, but autonomy. They created ROWE.

Results Only Work Environment is a management strategy where employees are evaluated on performance, not presence. In a ROWE, people focus on results and only results. In ROWE every person is free to do whatever they want, whenever they want, as long as the work gets done. In other words, work isn't a place you go, it's something you do.[58]

ROWE has had measurable results – it is not just a new fangled feel good strategy – it is a process and system, that when properly supported, makes a lot of sense. Here are a few of the benefits experienced by organizations that implemented ROWE:

Corporate Client:
- 17% increase in productivity
- 23% improvement in service quality
- 13% improvement in employee engagement

Local Government Agency:
- 9% increase in processing cases
- 77% decrease in unprocessed in-basket items

Retail Consulting Services Client:
- 100% increase in top line growth in less than 5 years

Manufacturing Client:
- Product delivery rate increased from 70% to 90%
- Time to build went from 50 hours to 35 hours

There are three primary pillars with a successful implementation of ROWE:

1. 13 directives or guideposts

2. a structured work-negotiation practice, and

3. the sludge eradication strategy

Examples of the 13 directives include:

"Every day feels like Saturday"

"It's okay to grocery shop on a Wednesday morning"

"People at all levels stop doing any activity that is a waste of their time, the customer's time or the company's money."

"Nobody talks about how many hours they work."

The structured work-negotiation practice

This is an agreement between the manager and the employee where three questions are asked, and answers agreed:

- What is being asked?
- When is it needed?
- What other communication will be required between now and then to get it done?

Sludge Eradication Strategy

When implementing ROWE, the developers Ressler and Thompson discovered that the biggest challenge with employees were their snarky comments and judgements of one another. For example, people would remark when someone left at 3:00, "Are you leaving early again today?" Ressler and Thompson called these comments "sludge." So, they created a "sludge" jar (like a swear jar) and every time someone said a judgmental comment, the offender had to put 50 cents in the jar. They developed a more in-depth program – this is just one example – they dubbed it the Environmental Sludge Eradication Strategy.

At Best Buy, ROWE was run as a pilot with great success. It was not long before other managers started asking for it. Ressler and Thompson let the program spread organically and by 2008 they had more than 80% of the employees operating as ROWE. This internally developed and organically grown program reduced voluntary turnover which saved the company millions of dollars. ROWE also resulted in higher productivity and improved employee wellbeing.

Author Cal Newport, who shared Best Buy's ROWE success story in a *New Yorker* article, wrote, "If you want to radically change when and where work happens in your organization while still achieving results, you also have to change the very definition of 'work' itself, moving it away from surveillance and visible busyness, and toward defined outcomes, trust and measurable results."[59]

Can you imagine ROWE in your own company? What would the photos look like in your workplace celebration album? I see focused, engaged employees, spending energy on work that they can invest their whole selves in, rather than expending energy ensuring they "look" the part with a butt in a seat so their manager can watch them.

Companies that are successful with ROWE invest in training. And, not just training with a light touch, vis a vis a onetime webinar and a playbook, but instead thoughtful and consistent training. The successful implementation of ROWE has leaders, managers and employees participating in ongoing training.

What would our world look like if more people felt autonomy and creativity with their work? If we use an asoebi approach, giving people the fabric they need and letting them tailor it for how they work best, what would that feel like? Our workplace album needs to include all of us – a range of ages, genders, ethnicities, and disabilities – both visible and invisible. What does a world of engaged people look like? How could it impact our communities and our societies?

Chances are you already have the components of an asoebi and ROWE approach to the workplace. Invite your employees to tailor a work approach that will also build community, ownership and belief in your company purpose. Doing so can result in greater employee engagement and higher productivity. It can also mean fewer days in a smaller office, bringing your business closer to net zero.

Circular Economy

A circular economy is based on the principles of designing out waste and pollution, keeping products and materials in use, and regenerating natural systems.[60] In contrast, a linear economy – how our economy has been run since the Industrial Revolution – is based upon take-make-waste: natural resources are taken from the ground, made into a product, and then discarded after being used up. Disrupting the linear system requires a transformation of all the elements of the current system: rethinking how resources are managed, made, used and what is done with the materials afterward. The goal of the circular economy is to create a system that can benefit everyone while considering the limits of our planet.

Celeste Tell is the founder of Epicycled, a company based upon the principles of circular economics. Epicycled designs, builds and operates workplace environments to increase agility while reducing capital, expense, time, disruption and waste throughout the full life cycle of a facility. Tell believes that the entire commercial office industry is centered on buying more stuff and getting rid of more stuff. For example, back in the 1990s when CRT (cathode-ray tube) monitors were popping up in offices, the furniture manufacturers fabricated large corner work surfaces to hold these very deep early monitors. These work surfaces eventually became obsolete as CRTs were replaced with slimmer flat screens. If the manufacturers projected forward a few years and imagined the end life cycle of the corner work surface, would they have come up with an adaptable solution so the furniture could evolve with the changing technology? Would they have used a material other than plastic laminate composite (Formica) that cannot be recycled?

Tell says, "We need to design for change." She shares that when you look at a typical project and consider the life cycles of the building, tenant improvements, furniture, equipment, and end-user, none of them align. In the commercial office industry, everything drives down to the lowest first cost with no consideration about the long-term impact. "That is just the way things have always been done," she laments.[61]

Office furniture manufacturer Ahrend has cracked this nut with the creation of furniture as a service (FAAS).[62] Ahrend already uses the principles of a circular economy with its manufacturing process and now, through their leasing program, they retain ownership of the furniture and use recovered components and materials to make the next chair, reducing future manufacturing costs. Ahrend's customers benefit through greatly reduced office set-up costs and greater flexibility around planning cycles, which are usually five to eight years, while furniture lasts much longer. This flexibility allows FAAS customers to have a current interior design that fits the needs of the brand and the employees and avoids the need for storage or production of waste as situations change.

Conscious Capitalism

For our own personal life choices, we might invest in a higher priced product that lasts longer or is less harmful to the environment, but that is not the case in the corporate world. So, it's important to ask the question: Who is incentivized to challenge the status quo? The commercial office industry is based upon size, comfort, and aversion to risk – all directly tied to American capitalism. And yet, even entrenched capitalists have another way to make a profit. Consider the founder of Patagonia, Yvon Chouinard, and how his approach emulates tenets of the Conscious Capitalism movement.

Chouinard started Patagonia in 1973 to make climbing gear he couldn't find anywhere else.[63] The mindset of his business was, "We are going to be here for 100 years. This company is the resource I have and I'm going to use that resource to show a different way of doing business." Patagonia evolved from designing and fabricating climbing equipment to become a clothing manufacturer. His "100 years" philosophy caused Chouinard to create a garment repair business to send the message to his customers that, "You don't throw things away, you repair them."

Patagonia has committed itself to owning the products it sells forever. If a customer buys a jacket and wants to get rid of it (whenever and for whatever reason) they will help sell it to someone else. If it needs mending, they will repair it. Or, if it totally breaks down, and is no longer useable, Patagonia will recycle it into another product. Patagonia's lifetime guarantee means that they do not make things cheaply.

(One of Patagonia's ads that caught my eye a couple of years ago said, "Dress Better. Save the Planet." I immediately substituted "work" for "dress" and this initial idea is one of the things that inspired me to further develop the 7 PLLANET tenets.)

Chouinard's company was founded before Conscious Capitalism became a movement, yet his philosophy aligns well with the four tenets of Conscious Capitalism, which is a movement co-founded by Raj Sisodia of Babson School of Business and John Mackey, CEO of Whole Foods. Conscious Capitalism is a way of thinking about capitalism and business that creates financial, social, cultural, emotional, spiritual, physical and ecological wealth for all stakeholders. There are four primary tenets of Conscious Capitalism: Higher Purpose, Stakeholder Orientation, Conscious Leadership and Conscious Culture.[64]

Higher Purpose – Elevating humanity through business begins with knowing why your company exists – businesses exist for reasons beyond just making a profit. Profit is a necessary means to achieve purpose, but not as an end in and of itself.

Stakeholder Orientation – A business needs to create value with and for its various stakeholders (customers, employees, vendors, investors, communities, etc.). Like the life forms in an ecosystem, healthy stakeholders lead to a healthy business environment.

Conscious Leadership – Conscious leaders understand and embrace the Higher Purpose of business and focus on creating value for and harmonizing with the interests of the business stakeholder. They recognize the integral role of culture and purposefully cultivate Conscious Culture.

Conscious Culture – The ethos – the values, principles, practices – underlying the social fabric of a business, which permeates the atmosphere of a business and connects the stakeholders to each other and to the purpose, people, and processes that comprise the company. All companies have a culture, but not all companies intentionally develop a culture that promotes their values and purpose.

Conscious Capitalism is a blueprint for doing as little harm as possible to the planet by making conscious decisions that positively impact people while making a profit. A natural progression for a business that chooses to operate using the four tenets of Conscious Capitalism is to become a certified B-Corp [65] or register as a Benefit Corporation.[66] There are numerous resources and books to learn more if you are interested in pursuing any of these avenues. I mention them because the philosophies of all these naturally tie into the 7 PLLANET tenets.

Chouinard shares that he is a student of Zen Buddhism and he profoundly believes in "the more you know, the less you need" approach to life. He is an avid fly fisherman and tried an experiment for a year, using the same fly every time he went out. He caught more fish than he ever had in his life in that one year with the same fly. Chouinard did not need all the other types of fancy flies – he just needed this one. Instead of messing around with a multitude of flies he spent time that year learning new lessons and techniques. Chouinard said, "Everything in your life pulls you to be more complex. When you go to a simpler life, it will not be an impoverished life. It will be really rich."[67]

Chouinard's words about fly fishing stayed with me. What would happen if organizations, instead of trying to make things more complex by leasing more space than they need, or purchasing the latest office furniture solution, were to first spend more time in conversations with their people? Conversations about improving processes, sharing knowledge, making how they work with each other more meaningful and efficient – connected to a higher purpose? It would not be an impoverished empty office life, and it could result in an immensely rewarding and rich place to work. This approach – a less is more mindset – is how the organization featured in the next case study approached their plan for a post-pandemic way of working.

Goal: **To create an inspiring culture with no physical location**

Headcount: **15**

The rapidly growing media agency had a physical office in a small town for its employees with a couple employees who traveled 60 minutes or more to get to the office. As the pandemic began shuttering offices in the spring of 2020, the agency's two partners recognized an opportunity to rethink the purpose of a physical office and consider how to maintain their vibrant team-based culture with employees working from home.

Purpose

The company's foundational values were honesty, authenticity, integrity and respect. They valued relationships and trust, and predominantly worked as a closely knit team. The partners' trust in their employees was one reason they were so inclusive in conversations with all staff about possible new ways of working.

Language

The team did not use words like "hybrid" or "remote" to describe how staff would work. Instead, they focused on the outcomes and expectations for delivering quality work. They determined that a results-only work environment (ROWE) aligned well with their values of honesty, authenticity, integrity and respect. Of course, for ROWE to work, the approach had to have a strong foundation of trust.

Less

With the ability to abandon its physical presence if it chose to, the agency realized it could get by with so much less: less real estate, less operating costs, less time commuting, less gas burned. Less was a strong component of this organization's decision to become a predominantly remote team. They let their lease expire on their office space and instead invested money in in-person gatherings every three months that could happen anywhere. This approach allowed them to create memorable team building experiences without the limitations of an office.

Ask

The team was inclusive from the get-go, with an anonymous survey, workshop for all employees, and encouraging ongoing input into the design of their in-person events. All ideas were welcome and as a result there was true ownership of the resulting meetings and events. The team also focused on the science of what makes a great team, especially one that is primarily virtual. They focused on the importance of social cohesion, information sharing and trust and created new processes that strengthened these factors.

Net Zero

Dramatically reducing commutes and eliminating a physical office were the greatest savings for the planet in this equation. Staff also shared tips with each other that they'd adopted in their own homes to reduce carbon footprints. The company was a model for how to do more with less and the business partners were inspired to become a certified B-corp as well.

Equity

The firm was relatively flat from an organizational structure, and that aspect is expected to continue as the firm grows. By becoming primarily remote they also have a tremendous opportunity to diversify their staff by no longer being limited by geographic boundaries. They also were sensitive to possible home office inequities as outlined in case study #2, and are prepared to offer accommodations to provide equity for remote workers.

Time

Clearly these leaders jumped at the chance the pandemic gave them to think differently. They recognized that it was an opportune time to reconsider the notion of an office and were willing to break new ground in their part of the world.

EQUITY

Although there are laws in place to protect against discrimination in hiring practices, the majority of physical workplaces have been designed from a singular viewpoint. Can you guess whose? Bingo! Our current working practices came directly from the white, heterosexual male-dominated Industrial Revolution, which, in turn, has influenced the physical design of offices. Included in this section are a few examples that show how things we take for granted as "the way things are" do not work for all people.

There has been a lot in the news about equity in the workplace, especially in the United States since the Black Lives Matter movement gained ground after George Floyd was murdered by a policeman in 2020 and the murder was witnessed on film by the world. Systemic racism has deep roots in the world of work and in the workplace, and inequities exist in ways you might not even imagine. Did you know that touchless sensors for restroom faucets and automatic doors with sensors have been calibrated for light skin?[68] It was a client who informed me of his experience at his office building – he shared that he hoped their new office would allow him to properly wash his hands. Such a basic, essential need – especially in a pandemic – that many light-skinned people most likely take for granted.

Diversity and Inclusion

Dr. S. Atiya Martin, CEM is a diversity, inclusion and equity transformation practitioner and is the author of *We Are The Question + The Answer: Break the Collective Habit of Racism + Build Resilience for Racial Equity in Ourselves and Our Organizations*. Dr. Martin shared with me, "There is a way that we need to be as an organization that facilitates inclusivity for everyone – we don't do that today. Everyone has to just come and fit. If we start from that place – a place where we want to be inclusive – then there are foundational things that organizations need to do for everybody that they are not doing now."[69] Dr. Martin believes we need to change our individual and organizational habits; changing the system means changing ourselves.

Dr. Martin told me that after George Floyd was murdered, she had all manners of company leaders reaching out to her asking how they could be more supportive. She responded to these inquiries with, "Have you asked them (your employees)? Why are you going outside your own organization?" Dr. Martin said, "There is this perception that there is one inclusive way to be." She went on, "It all connects – there is something about focusing on process and using it as a way to facilitate stealthy learning. Breakout groups report out on what the other person says and that can create moments that allow people to understand why something is important to them. The discussions normalize that we all have tendencies and habits and allows us to engage with more humanity and empathy."[70]

Physiology

If you see women with sweaters and gloves on in their office when it is 90 F degrees outside, you can chalk it up to a factory-set thermostat temperature standard based upon a man's metabolism.[71] Adjusting thermostats to be slightly warmer in the hot weather not only will ensure more comfort for all office occupants, but will lower energy costs and, potentially, help fight global warming.

Workplace restrooms may be designed for those with mobility impairments or who are wheelchair users because of the requirements of the *Americans With Disability Act Guidelines (ADAG)* in the United States, but they are not welcoming to all. The history of restroom design is based upon a singular view of biological and technical requirements and sex segregation.[72]

The ability to access restrooms that fit a person's identity is a rather basic human need. Our workplaces should have safe, sustainable, and inclusive public restrooms for everyone regardless of age, gender, race, religion, or disability. This design dilemma has been solved by a company that has developed a smart, efficient, inclusive public restroom solution called Stalled! Their design includes singular water closets (toilets) that one accesses regardless of gender identity and ensures that the typical visual gaps between restroom side panels and doors are sealed. The sinks and circulation areas are shared and accessible to all, helping to diffuse concerns about being alone and vulnerable. Stalled! is a solution worth exploring.[73] See *figure #19*

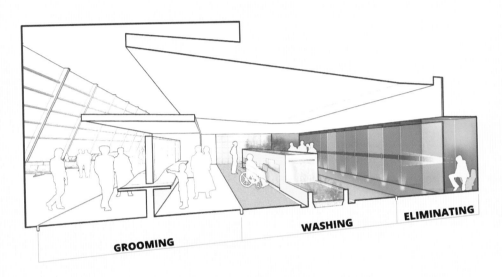

Figure #19: Stalled! Airport Restroom Prototype. Courtesy of JSA/MIXdesign.

Neurodiversity

There are recent initiatives focused on designing for neurodiversity as well as for race, gender and mobility. Neurodivergent conditions include Autism Spectrum Disorder (ASD, including Asperger Syndrome), Attention Deficit Hyperactivity Disorder (ADHD) and Dyslexia. Research shows that several factors in the workplace environment can negatively impact people with neurodivergence including poor acoustics, flickering lighting, chaotic space organization, odors, and confusing wayfinding (wayfinding means having clear signage and obvious pathways through an office). The good news is that the best practices for creating an inclusive work environment that support neurodivergent individuals include features that are beneficial to all workers: better acoustics, natural lighting, smart wayfinding, thermal comfort, and plentiful air ventilation.[74]

It has been reported that up to 17 percent of the population have been diagnosed with a neurodivergent condition:

- Four percent have ADD/ADHD
- One percent have Autism
- 10 percent have Dyslexia
- One percent have Dyspraxia
- One percent have Tourette Syndrome[75]

What are ways to create a work environment that is inclusive and supports neurodiversity? Pay attention to lighting, texture, color, wayfinding, noise, distractions, and interruptions. An excellent resource to reference is a comprehensive Sensory Environment Checklist that is available online at Neurodiversity and Buildings Checklist - BBC.[76]

A diverse workforce is a richer workforce, and that applies to neurodiversity as well. Proven out-of-the-box-thinker Richard Branson, CEO of Virgin, has said, "My dyslexia became my massive advantage: it helped me to think creatively and laterally, and see solutions where others saw problems."[77]

Architecture and design can build community with the resulting spaces. Think about how a well-designed public meeting forum supports healthy dialogue. Or, how a space with comfortable seating, located in a cozy corner with soft lighting and good acoustics can be a wonderful conversation nook for 4 people, allowing them to have a private and intimate conversation. It is not just with physical architectural design, but also through the process of discovery – through conversations and deliberate use of terms as explained in the Ask and Language chapters of this book – that we can connect people who are different from each other around shared values and purpose, building a more equitable and inclusive way of working.

A Solution for Equity in Housing and Working

Christelle Rohaut has a master's degree in city planning at Berkley. It was when she was there in 2016 studying the housing crisis, that she came up with the idea for Codi, a business that is considered a cross between Airbnb and WeWork. (Codi is a mash-up of the words "coworking" and "diversity.")

Rohaut was puzzled that people spend so much money for a space (their residence) that sits empty 8 or 9 hours a day while they are at work. She recognized that it is hugely inefficient to travel downtown to sit at a desk and leave a residential space vacant all day. She wondered if the living spaces could be used differently.

Rohaut has a city planner's mind and it bothered her that the residential real estate was only being used during the week from 6:00 PM to 8:00 AM – essentially for dinner and sleeping. She saw it as a waste. The idea that people should be able to walk to work and live in their neighborhood grew on her. She stopped seeing residential space as being used for only one purpose and instead viewed this space as a bit more complex, just as people are complex.

A millennial, Rohaut also recognized that the largest financial burden that she and her peers faced is paying their mortgage or rent. She saw that the further people lived away from their job, the less money they got paid – in turn a significant equity problem. She thought, "If one does not need to commute anymore, then it can create more equity in the workplace." Rohaut wants to create a walk to work revolution – having people walk to work every day.

Her model has homeowners renting out their residential spaces to be used as coworking spaces during the day to people who live close by. It is a model of "for local by local" meaning that anyone who uses the daytime spaces typically walks or bikes to the house. Of course, there are environmental benefits with less commuting, but there are economic benefits, too.

Less energy is used in offices with fewer people occupying them, and commuting is eliminated or reduced. According to Rouhat, every employee in the United States represents two tons of carbon emission annually, and they spend 240 hours a year of their life commuting. Remote workers can substantially reduce their carbon footprint: they can produce 40% fewer emissions, 32% less paper waste, and 20% less space and energy consumption when they work remotely.

The economic benefits include passive income for homeowners, which can help them pay their mortgage. This model also mimics the idea of satellite office spaces – allowing you to work close to where you live. Codi is now doing enterprise-wide configurations so that large corporations are able to establish satellite coworking spaces near where their desired talent (future and current) live. Rohaut commented, "We won't go back to an office-centric model and people are also afraid of the work from home-centric model – they don't want to be stuck at home every day, not seeing people and feeling isolated. When you go to a Codi space you will see others, still have a chance to socialize and connect, and learn from your peers. It is a community of remote workers in their own neighborhoods."[78]

Goal: **To create an inspiring work environment that builds community after a merger**

Employees: **180**

Two non-profits merged to consolidate efforts and be more powerful together. Naturally, each had its own culture coming into the merger. The desire was to create a shared experience that recognized the history and strengths of each organization and inspired staff to build authentic connections with each other.

Purpose

Each organization had similar mission statements and it was through the merger that they clarified their purpose to create a new statement: "To positively impact our community by making each other better." They found that this statement encouraged them to support each other within the new organization and extended naturally to citizens in the community who relied on their services.

Language

Mergers can be difficult. Careful language is especially important because people may fear their job is redundant. Tensions are often high because of the uncertainty of such a disruptive event. Therefore, the language used to describe the joining of the two organizations was framed with the word "combination" rather than "merger." From the beginning of discussions, the leaders made it very clear that each person's contributions made a difference, and their intention was to find a way to match an individual's talents with new opportunities. Although they could not guarantee jobs would not be eliminated, they made it clear that their goal was to find new opportunities and be open to employee suggestions for improvements.

Less

With the organization combination, two separate offices would no longer be required. They found a new office that was within a 30-mile radius of 70% of their employees' commutes. The new office was designed around agile (unassigned) seating and was approximately 50% smaller than the previous office of the largest entity. The physical space was very important to their mission, as they often host community gatherings and need to be accessible to public transportation for their clients. The organization also reduced commutes dramatically by encouraging staff to only come to the office when an in-person gathering was required, or if the office was a preferable environment to their home working situation. Finally, they used Codi, which allowed employees to walk or bike to a neighborhood coworking space located in a residence when they wanted to escape their own home office.

Ask

As soon as it was understood that the two organizations would combine, they began a series of focus group discussions and included all employees in the conversations. They held community listening sessions to hear what was most important to their clients and how the new office could support the community's needs. Many of the organization's clients speak English as a second language, so they translated materials into the six most spoken languages, and had interpreters present to translate back into English for those who only speak English.

Net Zero

Net Zero was a major driver of this organization and they made as many decisions as they could with the planet's health in mind. From reducing commutes, to choosing a highly energy-efficient building, increasing composting, reducing paper, encouraging lifestyle changes for employees, and continuously looking for ways to reduce their carbon footprint, this organization became a local beacon for how to work in the 21st century.

Equity

Through the early listening sessions with employees, they learned that some people did not feel comfortable in the workplace. They used the combination event as an opportunity to increase the sense of belonging by LGBTQ+ and Black employees and renewed their commitment to "make each other better."

Time

According to the executive director, who shared that the opportunity to merge came about relatively quickly, "We didn't know this was our time. But it was right on time." She is grateful that during the pandemic they worked efficiently and made impactful changes that will improve the community they serve, the people they employ, and ultimately the planet they inhabit.

TIME

NOW is the time to act to make essential changes to the way you work and to your physical workplace. COVID-19 gave us a gift-wrapped opportunity to question embedded assumptions about how things have always been done, to pause and reconsider a new way forward (not a "return to normal") and a chance to make impactful choices that will help us fight climate change. When discussing "time" in this section, the intention is twofold: the urgency of this moment in time to act and reconsidering the amount of time employees spend in the physical office.

The world of work has evolved a bit from the Industrial Revolution due to technology, but not as much as one would hope. 2020 gave us the most dramatic and disruptive shift to how we work since the introduction of desktop computers in the 1970s. The worldwide pandemic, social movements like Me Too and Black Lives Matter, alongside a rapidly heating climate, have given us opportunities to reconsider how we work and how we create places that support that work. As tragic as COVID-19 has been, this is the time to make radical, lasting, and sustainable changes.

The 9 to 5 Workday

During the Industrial Revolution and the decades that followed, hellish 16-hour workdays were pretty much the norm. It was Welsh social reformer Richard Owen who saw that this way of working was unsustainable and who began to campaign for the 8-hour workday. The uncomplicated rationale was that, of the 24 hours in a day, we should aim to split them equally between work, leisure, and rest.[79]

Henry Ford was among the first to introduce the 8-hour day into his company back in 1914. It proved to be a roaring success, in terms of both productivity and profitability. Other companies quickly followed suit. The Monday through Friday, 9 to 5 workday has not seriously been challenged since it was created.

Yet, working parents juggle children's needs when they are young, and manage their education as they enter school. Schools are still based upon an agrarian calendar when children were needed in the fields in the summer. School days also typically end two or three hours before many workdays, requiring after school childcare programs.

There is a misalignment between schooling, working, and parenting and it has been that way since the Industrial Revolution. Now is the time to challenge what the work week looks like and provide flexibility for when work happens.

Levels of stress, mental illness and opioid use have continued to increase over the past several decades. We are at the most medically advanced time in our history, yet our life expectancy has shrunk to its lowest level since the last world-wide pandemic in 1918, when there was also a world war raging.[80] How we work is so seriously broken and dysfunctional that we don't even see how bad it is because it is "normal."

People have used this time during the pandemic to reassess their priorities. Many have moved their families away from large cities to access better neighborhoods for their children, or to be closer to mountains or oceans to enjoy a higher quality of life. They have prioritized their health and wellbeing, using the time that had been spent on commuting to instead exercise, play with their kids, walk their dog or meditate. Hard driving over-achievers have realized that a bit more time with family makes them happier and less stressed. Employees are rejecting the idea of going back to normal if that means trekking into an office every day.

The employer who declares, "We will not go back, but instead will evolve and go forward" will be the real leader. Watch the number of employees who vote with their two feet and head to an organization that is willing to change and challenge the way things have always been done. When you can provide employees the flexibility they desire, not only will employees have better lives, but they will also perform at a higher level.

Employers that support employees with their life experience see a 23% increase in the number of employees reporting better mental health and a 17% increase in the number of employees reporting better physical health. Employers also see a 21% increase in the number of high performers compared to organizations that don't provide the same degree of support to their employees.[81]

Gartner's 2020 Reimagine HR Employee Survey revealed that only 36% of employees were high performers at organizations with a standard 40-hour work week. Organizations that offer employees flexibility over when, where and how much they work, see 55% of their work force as high performers.[82]

How can you make your employees' work lives and personal lives more balanced and harmonious? Try challenging how things have always been done by using a systematic approach to innovation – try the SIT model.

A systematic approach to innovation

There are as many methodologies and approaches to innovation as there are theories and models. One that I particularly like for innovation is called Systematic Inventive Thinking (SIT).

SIT is an organized, structured approach to idea generation. Rather than coming up with as many random ideas as possible (a traditional brainstorming approach), SIT uses the "Closed World" condition as its most important principle. Closed World simply means that everything you need exists within the problem or product in front of you. To find a solution you reorganize the existing objects or components using different thinking tools. This process has been used by senior level engineers and fourth grade students. It is taught at numerous universities and business schools worldwide, including Columbia, Duke and Wharton. It works, is fun to do, and has led to brilliant ideas ranging from the Sony Walkman to anesthesia devices used in operating rooms around the world.

Define The Problem

The first step in using SIT is to define the problem. Once the problem is defined, finding the solution simply requires reorganization of the existing building blocks. There are 5 thinking tools you can use in the SIT process: subtraction, multiplication, division, task unification and attribute dependency. For the purposes of this brief exercise, we will focus on subtraction only. For further explanation of all of the thinking tools, please reference *Inside The Box: A Proven System of Creativity for Breakthrough Results* by Drew Boyd and Jacob Goldenberg.

How to use the exercise: You can do this exercise as a group, or you can ask your colleagues to go through the exercise independently and then come together to share the results. It does not take long to do, and participants typically enjoy the process. There is no right "level" of hierarchy or job title to participate in this exercise. All that is needed is an open mind and a willingness to try something new. Everyone, from janitorial and maintenance staff to global VPs, could be invited to participate. Even better, include colleagues from other departments like IT and HR to build cross departmental connections. Sometimes the most innovative idea comes from the least expected source.

To start: Define the problem and list all the parts of the problem. Share this information with your team and invite them to add any missing parts – they may recognize pieces or components you did not capture. For this example, we will use the process of occupancy planning an office environment for an organization that is implementing hybrid working. 80% of employees will be in the office 2-3 days/week; 10% in office 5 days/week; 10% will remain remote.

1. **List the product's or service's internal components (e.g., all the parts of the problem or product**

   • Workstation/desk   • Days of the week
   • Chair   • Time of the day
   • Employee headcount

2. **Select an essential component and imagine removing it.**
   There are two ways:

   A. Full Subtraction. The entire component is removed

   B. Partial Subtraction. Take one of the features or functions of the components away or diminish it in some way. For this example, let's go with full subtraction and remove the workstation/desk component

3. **Visualize the resulting concept** (no matter how strange it seems). We are left with planning an office without workstations/desks.

4. **Ask:** What are the potential benefits and values? Who would want this new product or service and why would they find it valuable? If you are trying to solve a particular problem, how can it help address that challenge?

   We have chairs, heads, days of the week and time of the day, but no workstations. Who would want this type of space? What value would it have to an organization? How could it impact occupancy planning?

I'll pause this exercise to share a conversation held recently with a client. The CEO of a global media agency was reflecting on how COVID-19 will impact her organization's work and the workplace in the future. "When COVID-19 turned the world upside down, it also showed us what is possible. The office is a giant convention waiting to be disrupted. From a place to do work to a destination that brings us together for learning, team building, collaboration, and engagement. I imagine a place for learning, meeting spaces with collaboration technology, small huddle rooms and far fewer desks."

A space that is full of people gathering to collaborate, learn, and connect – the type of space that results from subtracting workstations – is exactly what this CEO wants.

5. **Ask again:** If you decide this new product or service is valuable, then ask, Is it feasible? Can you actually create these new products? Perform these new services? Why or why not? Is there any way to refine or adapt the idea to make it more viable?

Once you have completed the exercise, ask yourself and your team where you can apply these ideas in your own work that might have meaningful impact. How can you help your organization perform better, reduce expenses, and contribute to the organizational mission in ways that makes you and your team a key business partner?

In the example above, the media agency created a student union style workplace full of cozy lounge areas, a library zone, coffee-collaboration spaces, and a variety of meeting spaces. There were a few desks to be used as touch-down spaces between meetings, but there were far fewer desks than in the previous configuration.

Figure #20: When at least 25% of people change their social behavior, the majority will follow their example.

The Tipping Point

Research shows that a small amount of people (estimated at 8%) will change their habits because it is the right thing to do – because they feel morally obligated.[83] Yet, to make a positive difference on climate change, we need many more to move in a different direction. The good news is that the tipping point for social change is not a simple majority of 51%; in fact, it is 25%.[84] Social behavior change research shows that, as Margaret Mead said many years ago, a small group of committed people can make a difference.

"Never doubt that a small group of thoughtful, committed citizens can change the world. Indeed, it is the only thing that ever has." – Margaret Mead

---

Some of the topics shared in the 7 PLLANET tenets are not for the faint of heart. NOW is the time to be inclusive, bold, thoughtful, and courageous, but you only need to be in the committed 25% to begin working towards challenging the status quo. Others will follow your lead. And, if we work fast, we may have a fighting chance of stalling climate change.

Goal: **To chart a new direction for long term growth**

Employees: **5000**

The company, founded in the early 1900s, is a major utility provider. A new CEO took the helm just as the pandemic was sending people home for remote working. The new leader was interested in continuing the strong growth experienced under the previous leadership. Although a very experienced leader, this was her first time serving as CEO.

Purpose

The organizational purpose is to create a better future by reimaging energy for people and the planet. This bold purpose statement was made more concrete by the new CEO through her early conversations and listening sessions. She intentionally focused on how the company could create a better future for the world through bold actions.

Language

The former beloved CEO had a strong relationship with, and was well respected by, staff. The new CEO recognized employees were feeling a sense of loss with his departure. She chose her words carefully when talking with employees in one-on-one conversations and in focus group sessions. She called these "listening sessions" and did just that – saying very little as she listened to their ideas, frustrations, and suggestions. She did not hold any Town Halls for the first six months and instead took time to visit with small groups of employees every week.

Less

Coming from an organization that had embraced activity-based seating, the new CEO recognized that the 1990s headquarters was stuck in the past. C-suite offices were 400 to 500 square feet each. High walled workstations were 80 to 100 square feet. She made it a goal to show staff how they could dramatically reduce their office footprint, while providing a much more dynamic and interactive workspace. She committed to reducing their physical office footprint by at least 60%.

Ask

The CEO was bold in her approach: she invited more than the senior leaders into conversations with her. She purposefully included front line workers, linemen and truck drivers because she wanted to understand what they dealt with every day. In the listening sessions with employees the CEO asked two specific questions. 1) What are we doing really well that we should continue doing? 2) What are we doing that we should stop doing? A strong believer in possibilities, the CEO asked each employee to write a letter to their future self in 5 years, envisioning how the world would change for the better because of their focus, passion and hard work.

Net-Zero

The company made a pledge to become a net zero company by 2050 or sooner, and to also help the world get to net zero. They committed to install methane measurement at all their major oil and gas process sites by 2023 and to reduce methane intensity of operations by 50%. They focused on how they could fundamentally transform the whole organization and maintain their commitment to performing while transforming.

Equity

The company focused on ways to improve their benefits to all employees. Spousal health insurance had been available to same-sex couples and non-traditional families for several years, but their parental policy could be improved. They adopted an inclusive, 16-week paid parental leave policy that extends to parents regardless of gender, or if they are primary or secondary caregivers. (Often mothers are assumed to be the primary caregiver and receive more generous benefits.) The policy covers birth, adoption, and foster care. The CEO shared, "This is good for our bottom line in terms of employee engagement and retention. Giving someone the opportunity to invest in their family at critical points in their lives keeps them engaged, loyal and employed."

Time

It certainly was a difficult time – in the middle of a pandemic – to step in as a new CEO. Yet, she saw this as a chance to be a fearless leader in a traditionally conservative organization to make a positive difference – in a fossil fuel industry, no less – on climate change. She honored the company's past and its legacy but stayed steadfast on her goal of making a positive difference for her people and the planet.

CONCLUSION

Historically, pandemics have forced humans to break with the past and imagine their world anew. This one is no different. It is a portal, a gateway between one world and the next. We can choose to walk through it, dragging the carcasses of our prejudice and hatred, our avarice, our data banks and dead ideas, our dead rivers, and smoky skies behind us. Or we can walk through lightly, with little luggage, ready to imagine another world. And ready to fight for it.
—Arundhati Roy, Financial Times, April 4, 2020.

Our offices and business working practices were broken well before COVID-19. The pandemic, as tragic as it has been, can be viewed as providing a valuable opportunity to rethink the purpose of the office and reconsider how we work, so we can make positive changes for our own wellbeing and for the health of the planet.

The time is now to have conversations with your leaders, managers and employees about work and the workplace. Employees have been left out of these conversations for far too long. Bringing them into the conversation is a crucial step to meaningful change.

Research shows that only 8% of people will change their habits because it is the right thing to do – because they feel morally obligated. Yet, to make a positive difference on climate change, we need many more to move in a different direction. As discussed, the good news is that the tipping point for social change is not a simple majority; in fact, it is 25%.

Building a workplace disruption movement requires leadership – courageous leadership. If you have reached this point in the book, then I believe you are a leader who wants to make a difference, to leave your mark, and to disrupt how things have been done to make smarter decisions for the planet. You now know what you need to do.

It requires courage to reconsider the notion of work and the workplace. A willingness to challenge the status quo, beginning with an examination of your own vision and purpose. It takes bravery to speak up and question embedded assumptions. And a desire to imagine possibilities for new ways of working.

Let's get to work!

ACKNOWLEDGEMENTS

Thank you to my editor, Dionne McCulloch, whose guidance and input was invaluable and who inspired me to push through when the pushing got tough.

Thank you to Robert Brochu, my good friend and uber-talented graphic designer, who not only enriches our clients' projects with story walls and graphic design but created the interior design, illustrations, and cover for this book.

Thank you to early readers for giving me feedback that helped shape the final version, although all errors are solely my own: Amy King, Caren Martin, PhD, Cynthia Milota, Elizabeth Ross Holmstrom, Karen Plum, Lael Couper Jepson, Polly Chandler, and Robert Brochu.

Thank you to Atyia Martin, PhD, Celeste Tell, Christelle Rohaut, Mike Doehla, and Pious Ali for generously sharing their perspectives and stories with me.

Thank you to Kate Lister for her wisdom and guidance.

Thank you to my colleagues at Advanced Workplace Associates (AWA) who continually inspire me with their passion to make the world of work better. Extra gratitude to Chris Hood, whose enthusiastic environmental workplace activism knows no bounds.

Thank you to my clients over the years, both at Workplace Transformation Facilitation and AWA, who have given me the opportunity to refine my approach and have been willing to include all of their employees in the change process, so their voices are heard.

A note about Fritz Steele, PhD, in whose memory this book is dedicated.

Fritz was a pioneer in the fields of organizational development, change management, and organizational ecology. A prolific author of at least 12 books, Fritz authored *The Sense of Place* (1981) and co-authored *Workplace by Design* with Franklin Becker (1993). Those books greatly influenced my professional approach early in my career. When I learned that Fritz had moved to Maine a few years ago, I quickly tracked him down and introduced myself as one of his biggest fans. Fritz encouraged me to write. He mentored me for several years as I worked to figure out the book inside me. Fritz died in February 2020 and will be forever missed.

ABOUT THE AUTHOR

Lisa Whited believes in the art of possibility. She has a passion for improving processes and workplaces. Lisa has a holistic outlook on work: it has a ripple effect on our communities, society, and the planet. She is a change management strategist who is driven to make a dent in the abysmal Gallup statistic that 80% of people worldwide are disengaged at work.

Lisa has an MS in Organization and Management from Antioch University and holds certifications in mediation, facilitation, and interior design. She speaks and writes about the future of work, building community, and ensuring all voices are heard in a change process. Lisa consults with companies large and small, local, and global. Her recent engagements have been helping leaders figure out what the future of work will look like in a post-COVID-19 world.

Lisa and her husband, Pete Chanis, have three children, two cats and one dog and live in Portland, Maine.

ENDNOTES

[1] "State of the Global Workplace Report." Gallup.com, Gallup, 20 Nov. 2021, https://www.gallup.com/workplace/349484/state-of-the-global-workplace.aspx.

[2] Harrabin, Roger. "Climate Change: Young People Very Worried - Survey." BBC News, BBC, 14 Sept. 2021, https://www.bbc.com/news/world-58549373.

[3] Survey results for private client, January-November 2019.

[4] Aberge, Thibaut, et al. "Global Status Report 2017." Www.worldgbc.org, United Nations Environment Programme, 14 Sept. 2017, https://www.worldgbc.org/sites/default/files/UNEP%20188_GABC_en%20%28web%29.pdf.

[5] IPCC, 2021: Climate Change 2021: The Physical Science Basis. Contribution of Working Group I to the Sixth Assessment Report of the Intergovernmental Panel on Climate Change [Masson-Delmotte, V., P. Zhai, A. Pirani, S.L. Connors, C. Péan, S. Berger, N. Caud, Y. Chen, L. Goldfarb, M.I. Gomis, M. Huang, K. Leitzell, E. Lonnoy, J.B.R. Matthews, T.K. Maycock, T. Waterfield, O. Yelekçi, R. Yu, and B. Zhou (eds.)]. Cambridge University Press. In Press. Accessed 15 Aug. 2021, https://www.ipcc.ch/report/ar6/wg1/.

6 IPCC, 2021: Climate Change 2021: The Physical Science Basis. Contribution of Working Group I to the Sixth Assessment Report of the Intergovernmental Panel on Climate Change [Masson-Delmotte, V., P. Zhai, A. Pirani, S.L. Connors, C. Péan, S. Berger, N. Caud, Y. Chen, L. Goldfarb, M.I. Gomis, M. Huang, K. Leitzell, E. Lonnoy, J.B.R. Matthews, T.K. Maycock, T. Waterfield, O. Yelekçi, R. Yu, and B. Zhou (eds.)]. Cambridge University Press. In Press. Accessed 15 Aug. 2021, https://www.ipcc.ch/report/ar6/wg1/.

7 Turrentine, Jeff. "IPCC: We've Already Warmed the Planet to Catastrophic Effect, but the Level of That Catastrophe Is up to Us." NRDC, 9 Aug. 2021, https://www.nrdc.org/stories/ipcc-weve-already-warmed-planet-catastrophic-effect-level-catastrophe-us?gclid=CjwKCAjw4qCKBhAVEiwAkTYsPMmSj6x7-J4CgBnz8zFT8MTmkvZ_S4IKAAqloGevDA5c5orgZ4w-MhoCqpMQAvD_BwE

8 Herman Miller Space Utilization Services. Accessed 21 Feb. 2021, https://www.hermanmiller.com/it_it/content/dam/hermanmiller/documents/research_topics/SpaceUtl.pdf.

9 Aberge, Thibaut, et al. "Global Status Report 2017." Www.worldgbc.org, United Nations Environment Programme, 14 Sept. 2017, https://www.worldgbc.org/sites/default/files/UNEP%20188_GABC_en%20%28web%29.pdf.

10 "Workplace Stress." The American Institute of Stress, 9 Feb. 2021, https://www.stress.org/workplace-stress.

11 "History." The American Institute of Stress, 23 June 2020, https://www.stress.org/about/history.

12 "Workplace Stress." The American Institute of Stress, 9 Feb. 2021, https://www.stress.org/workplace-stress.

13 "Workplace Stress." The American Institute of Stress, 9 Feb. 2021, https://www.stress.org/workplace-stress.

14 "Daily Life." The American Institute of Stress, 18 Dec. 2019, https://www.stress.org/daily-life.

15 "Loss Aversion." BehavioralEconomics.com | The BE Hub, 14 Oct. 2020, https://www.behavioraleconomics.com/resources/mini-encyclopedia-of-be/loss-aversion/.

[16] Miller, Kelsey. "5 Critical Steps in the Change Management Process: HBS Online." Business Insights Blog, 19 March 2020, https://online.hbs.edu/blog/post/change-management-process.

[17] Tasler, Nick. "Stop Using the Excuse 'Organizational Change Is Hard.'" Harvard Business Review, 31 Aug. 2021, https://hbr.org/2017/07/stop-using-the-excuse-organizational-change-is-hard?registration=success.

[18] Clift, Cortney. "It Will Get Easier." Medium, Elemental, 20 April 2020, https://elemental.medium.com/it-will-get-easier-30d90976b260#:~:text=%E2%80%9CWe%20have%20to%20remind%20ourselves,the%20day%20we%20were%20born.%E2%80%9D.

[19] Pink, Daniel H., and Daniel H. Pink. Drive: The Surprising Truth about What Motivates US. Canongate Books Ltd, 2018.

[20] Zander, Rosamund Stone, and Benjamin Zander. The Art of Possibility. Harvard Business School Press, 2000.

[21] Wertz, Jia. "Open-Plan Work Spaces Lower Productivity and Employee Morale." Forbes, Forbes Magazine, 1 July 2019, https://www.forbes.com/sites/jiawertz/2019/06/30/open-plan-work-spaces-lower-productivity-employee-morale/?sh=310373c961cd.

[22] Feintzeig, Rachel. "Study: Open Offices Are Making Us All Sick." The Wall Street Journal, Dow Jones & Company, 25 Feb. 2014, https://www.wsj.com/articles/BL-ATWORKB-1615.

[23] Newport, Cal. Deep Work: Rules for Focused Success in a Distracted World, Grand Central Publishing, New York, NY, 2016, pp. 3

[24] Grimando, Christine. "Portlands-Plan-2030." City of Portland, 2017. https://www.portlandmaine.gov/DocumentCenter/View/18271/Portlands-Plan-2030.

[25] Shinnan, Stephen. "Just How Fair Is Remote Work? A Question of Equity." WorkTango Inc, 16 Feb. 2021, https://worktango.com/2020/12/05/just-how-fair-is-remote-work/.

[26] Atske, Sara, and Andrew Perrin. "Home Broadband Adoption, Computer Ownership Vary by Race, Ethnicity in the U.S." Pew Research Center, Pew Research Center, 10 Sept. 2021, https://www.pewresearch.org/fact-tank/2021/07/16/home-broadband-adoption-computer-ownership-vary-by-race-ethnicity-in-the-u-s/.

[27] Shinnan, Stephen. "Just How Fair Is Remote Work? A Question of Equity." WorkTango Inc, 16 Feb. 2021, https://worktango.com/2020/12/05/just-how-fair-is-remote-work/.

[28] Workplace 2021: Appraising Future-Readiness - Leesman. https://www.leesmanindex.com/media/Leesman-Workplace-2021-Report-1.pdf.

[29] Lister, Kate, and Anita Kamouri. "Work from Home Experience Survey Results." Global Workplace Analytics, 8 Oct. 2021, https://globalworkplaceanalytics.com/global-work-from-home-experience-survey#AboutSurvey.

[30] Steelcase Global Report Changing Expectations and the ... Jan. 2021, https://www.steelcase.com/content/uploads/2021/02/2021_AM_SC_Global-Report_Changing-Expectations-and-the-Future-of-Work-2.pdf.

[31] Alexander, Andrea, et al. What Executives Are Saying about the Future of Hybrid Work. McKinsey & Company, 28 Aug. 2021, https://www.mckinsey.com/business-functions/people-and-organizational-performance/our-insights/what-executives-are-saying-about-the-future-of-hybrid-work#:~:text=In%20the%20postpandemic%20future%20of,executives%20across%20industries%20and%20geographies.&text=1.

[32] IEA, International Energy Association. "Energy Efficiency – Topics." IEA, 1 Nov. 2021, https://www.iea.org/topics/energy-efficiency.

[33] "International House Sizes." International House Sizes, Accessed 8 May 2021, http://demographia.com/db-intlhouse.htm.

[34] Published by Statista Research Department, and Jan 20. "Average Family Size in the US 1960-2020." Statista, 20 Jan. 2021, https://www.statista.com/statistics/183657/average-size-of-a-family-in-the-us/.

[35] "International House Sizes." International House Sizes, Accessed 8 May 2021, http://demographia.com/db-intlhouse.htm.

[36] Guy, Paula. Families and Households - Office for National Statistics, Office for National Statistics, 2 Mar. 2021, https://www.ons.gov.uk/peoplepopulationandcommunity/birthsdeathsandmarriages/families/datasets/familiesandhouseholdsfamiliesandhouseholds.

[37] Unused Space in Buildings Generates 22m Tons of CO2." Defining Standards for Counting People - Density Occupancy Systems, Accessed 10 May 2021. https://www.density.io/blog/how-companies-can-take-climate-action-with-occupancy-data.

[38] Susanka, Sarah, and Kira Obolensky. The Not so Big House: A Blueprint for the Way We Really Live. Taunton, 2009.

[39] Herman Miller Space Utilization Services. Accessed 11 March 2021, https://www.hermanmiller.com/it_it/content/dam/hermanmiller/documents/research_topics/SpaceUtl.pdf.

[40] PricewaterhouseCoopers. "Business Needs a Tighter Strategy for Remote Work." PwC, 12 Jan. 2021, https://www.pwc.com/us/en/library/covid-19/us-remote-work-survey.html.

[41] Block, Peter. "Invitation." Community: The Structure of Belonging, Berrett-Koehler Publishers, Incorporated, San Francisco, CA, 2008, pp. 113–122.

[42] Bernstein, Lenny. "U.S. Life Expectancy Declines Again, a Dismal Trend Not Seen since World War I." The Washington Post, WP Company, 29 Nov. 2018, https://www.washingtonpost.com/national/health-science/us-life-expectancy-declines-again-a-dismal-trend-not-seen-since-world-war-i/2018/11/28/ae58bc8c-f28c-11e8-bc79-68604ed88993_story.html.

[43] Ahmad, Kaitlin. "Fewer Americans Are Volunteering and Giving than Any..." UMD Right Now, 12 Jul. 2019, https://umdrightnow.umd.edu/fewer-americans-are-volunteering-and-giving-any-time-last-two-decades.

[44] "Interactive Presentation Software." Mentimeter, Accessed 12 Feb. 2021, https://www.mentimeter.com/.

[45] "Meeting Collaboration Platform." MeetingSift, Accessed 12 Feb. 2021, http://meetingsift.com/.

[46] Cain, Susan. Quiet: The Power of Introverts in a World That Can't Stop Talking. Crown Publishing, 2012.

[47] Pink, Daniel. "Is Purpose Really an Effective Motivator?: Daniel H. Pink." Daniel H. Pink | The Official Site of Author Daniel Pink, 29 March 2010, https://www.danpink.com/2010/03/is-purpose-really-an-effective-motivator/.

[48] Anders, George. "Employers Catch on: Remote Job Posts Rise 357% as Tech, Media Lead the Way." LinkedIn, LinkedIn, 9 Aug. 2021, https://www.linkedin.com/pulse/employers-catch-remote-job-posts-rise-457-tech-media-lead-anders/.

[49] Ali, Pious. Personal interview. 21 Feb. 2021.

[50] Doehla, Mike. Personal interview. 18 Feb. 2021.

51 Puzio, Angelica. "Who Wants to Return to the Office?" FiveThirtyEight, FiveThirtyEight, 11 Aug. 2021, https://fivethirtyeight.com/features/why-post-pandemic-offices-could-be-whiter-and-more-male/.

52 Newport, Cal. "How to Achieve Sustainable Remote Work." The New Yorker, 9 July 2021, https://www.newyorker.com/culture/cultural-comment/how-to-achieve-sustainable-remote-work.

53 EPA, Environmental Protection Agency, Accessed 8 Aug. 2021, https://www.epa.gov/facts-and-figures-about-materials-waste-and-recycling/durable-goods-product-specific-data#FurnitureandFurnishings.

54 EPA, Environmental Protection Agency, Accessed 15 Sept. 2021, https://www.epa.gov/transportation-air-pollution-and-climate-change/carbon-pollution-transportation#:~:text=Transportation%20and%20Climate%20Change,-Burning%20fossil%20fuels&text=%E2%80%8BGreenhouse%20gas%20(GHG)%20emissions,contributor%20of%20U.S.%20GHG%20emissions.

55 Lister, Kate, and Anita Kamouri. "Work from Home Experience Survey Results." Global Workplace Analytics, 8 Oct. 2021, https://globalworkplaceanalytics.com/global-work-from-home-experience-survey#AboutSurvey.

56 "Statistics on Remote Workers That Will Surprise You (2022)." Apollo Technical LLC, 16 Jan. 2022, https://www.apollotechnical.com/statistics-on-remote-workers/.

57 "Statistics on Remote Workers That Will Surprise You (2022)." Apollo Technical LLC, 16 Jan. 2022, https://www.apollotechnical.com/statistics-on-remote-workers/.

58 "Go Rowe." Go ROWE, Accessed 15 Aug. 2021, https://www.gorowe.com/.

59 Newport, Cal. "How to Achieve Sustainable Remote Work." The New Yorker, 9 July 2021, https://www.newyorker.com/culture/cultural-comment/how-to-achieve-sustainable-remote-work.

60 "New to Circular Economy Overview." Ellen MacArthur Foundation, Accessed 9 Aug. 2021, https://ellenmacarthurfoundation.org/topics/circular-economy-introduction/overview.

61 Tell, Celeste. Personal interview. 12 March 2021.

62 "Bringing Office Furniture Full Circle: Ahrend." How to Build a Circular Economy, Accessed 9 Aug. 2021, https://ellenmacarthurfoundation.org/circular-examples/bringing-office-furniture-full-circle.

63 "Patagonia: Yvon Chouinard." NPR, NPR, 25 Dec. 2017, https://www.npr.org/2018/02/06/572558864/patagonia-yvon-chouinard.

64 "Our Philosophy." Conscious Capitalism, 24 Aug. 2021, https://www.consciouscapitalism.org/philosophy.

65 "B Corp Certification Demonstrates a Company's Entire Social and Environmental Impact." B Corp Certification Demonstrates a Company's Entire Social and Environmental Impact., Accessed 28 Aug. 2021, https://www.bcorporation.net/en-us/certification/.

66 "Benefit Corporation." How to Become a Benefit Corporation | Benefit Corporation, Accessed 28 Aug. 2021, https://benefitcorp.net/businesses/how-become-benefit-corporation.

67 "Patagonia: Yvon Chouinard." NPR, NPR, 25 Dec. 2017, https://www.npr.org/2018/02/06/572558864/patagonia-yvon-chouinard.

68 Gronneberg, Bethlehem. "'What Does Tech Have to Do with It?': Everything. the Case for Diversity of Thoughts." Fargo INC! Magazine, 14 July 2020, https://www.fargoinc.com/what-does-tech-have-to-do-with-it-everything-the-case-for-diversity-of-thoughts/.

69 Martin, PhD, S. Atyia. Personal interview. 12 July 2021.

70 Martin, S. Atyia. We Are the Question + the Answer: Break the Collective Habit of Racism + Build Resilience for Racial Equity in Ourselves and Our Organizations. All Aces Publishing, 2021.

71 Belluck, Pam. "Chilly at Work? Office Formula Was Devised for Men." The New York Times, The New York Times, 3 Aug. 2015, https://www.nytimes.com/2015/08/04/science/chilly-at-work-a-decades-old-formula-may-be-to-blame.html.

72 "Historical Context." Stalled!, Accessed 22 March 2021, https://www.stalled.online/historicalcontext.

73 "Design." Stalled!, Accessed 22 March 2021, https://www.stalled.online/design.

74 Sargent, Kay, et al. "Designing a Neurodiverse Workplace." HOK, 30 Sept. 2020, https://www.hok.com/ideas/publications/hok-designing-a-neurodiverse-workplace/.

75 Sargent, Kay. "Designing for Neurodiversity and Inclusion." Work Design Magazine, 13 May 2020, https://www.workdesign.com/2019/12/designing-for-neurodiversity-and-inclusion/.

76 BBC UX&D Building Checklist, https://bbc.github.io/uxd-cognitive/

77 Osborne, Samuel. "Richard Branson: Being Dyslexic Is a Sign of Huge Intelligence." The Independent, Independent Digital News and Media, 1 May 2017, https://www.independent.co.uk/news/people/dyslexia-richard-branson-potential-intelligence-genius-advantage-virgin-a7710676.html.

78 Rohaut, Christelle. Personal interview. 1 March 2021.

79 Bryom, Matt. "Workday Shift: Is 9-5 Working Obsolete?" Business.com, 7 Oct. 2015, https://www.business.com/articles/the-death-of-the-workday-is-9-to-5-working-obsolete/.

80 Bernstein, Lenny. "U.S. Life Expectancy Declines Again, a Dismal Trend Not Seen since World War I." The Washington Post, WP Company, 29 Nov. 2018, https://www.washingtonpost.com/national/health-science/us-life-expectancy-declines-again-a-dismal-trend-not-seen-since-world-war-i/2018/11/28/ae58bc8c-f28c-11e8-bc79-68604ed88993_story.html.

81 Kropp, Brian. "9 Trends That Will Shape Work in 2021 and Beyond." Harvard Business Review, 30 April 2021, https://hbr.org/2021/01/9-trends-that-will-shape-work-in-2021-and-beyond.

82 Kropp, Brian. "9 Trends That Will Shape Work in 2021 and Beyond." Harvard Business Review, 30 April 2021, https://hbr.org/2021/01/9-trends-that-will-shape-work-in-2021-and-beyond.

83 Centola, Damon. The 25 Percent Tipping Point for Social Change ... 28 May 2019, https://www.psychologytoday.com/us/blog/how-behavior-spreads/201905/the-25-percent-tipping-point-social-change.

84 Houser Kristin Houser, Kristin. "How Many People Do You Need to Change the World? Here's the Breakdown." World Economic Forum, 12 June 2018, https://www.weforum.org/agenda/2018/06/want-to-change-society-s-views-here-s-how-many-people-you-ll-need-on-your-side/.

Printed in the USA
CPSIA information can be obtained
at www.ICGtesting.com
LVHW070553081123
763302LV00030B/16